SIX-GUN IN CHEEK

BILL PRONZINI

SIX-GUN IN CHEEK

AN AFFECTIONATE GUIDE TO THE "WORST" IN WESTERN FICTION

DOVER PUBLICATIONS, INC.
MINEOLA, NEW YORK

Bibliographical Note

This Dover edition, first published in 2017, is an unabridged republication of the work originally published by Crossover Press, Minneapolis, Minnesota, in 1997.

International Standard Book Number

ISBN-13: 978-0-486-82034-7
ISBN-10: 0-486-82034-3

Manufactured in the United States by LSC Communications
82034301   2017
www.doverpublications.com

Dedication

Rather than my dedicating this book to anyone or anything, I'm going to let a pair of Western-novel inscriptions, both by Nelson Nye in 1944, serve instead. Nothing I could come up with would be more fitting here than these.

For　　　　—a great hand with the organ.—CARTRIDGE-CASE
LAW

For my long-suffering wife—who deserves it.—WILD HORSE
SHORTY

Dedication

Acknowledgments

The credit (or blame) for Six-Gun in Cheek is not mine alone. A number of others helped in one way or another to bring it about, and so deserve recognition (or censure), too. My sincere thanks to:

Bruce Taylor and Steve Stilwell, whose mostly gentle nagging over a five-year-period finally produced the desired results;

Marcia Muller, my long-suffering wife (who doesn't deserve it), for putting up with all the cackles, howls, and out-loud recitals produced during my research; and

Bob Adey, Robert E. Briney, Lawrence Davidson, William F. Deeck, Arthur Hackathorn, Francis M. Nevins, Jr., James Pepper, Dale Walker, Jeff Wallmann, and Gene Zombolas, who provided nuggets, suggestions, books and magazines, and/or encouragement.

Contents

Contents

SIX-GUN IN CHEEK

Knighthood's still in flower. For, riding the crest of popularity at the present time, as never before in its long and glorious history, is the Western story.

On that grim dark day when romantic literature perishes, the soul of man shall perish, too. But as long as ideals are cherished; as long as stark courage engenders shining admiration in the heart; as long as men have splendid creeds to which their lives are pledged, Romance, a Joan of Arc in glittering armor, shall roam the earth.

The savage satire of Don Quixote failed to slay her, and the modern realists whose pens are held in far unsteadier fingers than those of Cervantes cannot prevail.... For the Western story is America's saga of chivalry. It is Uncle Sam's contribution to high adventure.

—Leo Margulies, Introduction to WESTERN THRILLERS (1935)

Preface: Slicker 'n Slobbers

When some people first learn of my extensive collection of Western fiction, they wrinkle their snouts and ask me why I collect *that* sort of thing. As if Westerns carry a social stigma that puts them in the same class with pornography and/or romantic nurse novels.

These scoffers and sneerers, these snooty types who look down their noses at Westerns, all seem to have one thing in common: None of them has ever read one. Nor do they know anything *about* Western fiction.

Such ignorance is not bliss. So I sit them down and educate them.

In the first place, I tell them, the Western story—as Leo Margulies says in the passage quoted above—is a uniquely American art form, one of the relative few (hard-boiled crime fiction is another) this country can call its own. It was born more than a hundred years ago with the dime novels of Ned Buntline and Colonel Prentiss Ingraham, and was later refined and given permanent literary stature by Mark Twain, Bret Harte, O. Henry, and Owen Wister, among others. During this century Western fiction has functioned as a symbol of all that America stands for: freedom, justice, self-reliance, the pioneer spirit. And in a century that has produced two world wars, dozens of localized wars and "police actions," the Great Depression, and other tragedies large and small, Americans have needed that spirit to sustain them.

In the second place, I tell these unenlightened folk, the popular image of the Western as Roy Rogers and Gene Autry juvenalia is largely bunkum. There are as many good, intelligent Western stories as any other type; and the best of them not only have literary and entertainment value, but function as education tools, providing the reader with information about—and insights into—the lives and accomplishments of the men and women who settled the western half of the U.S.

In the third place, I say to the poor ignorant souls, few things reveal more about a generation than its popular culture. If you were to examine a cross-section of Western fiction published during each decade of the 20th century, it would not only tell you what type of books and stories were read and who wrote them, but would provide details on moral, religious, and political attitudes, passions and prejudices, fads and fancies. Mini social histories of each decade, in fact, through which you could accurately assess the progression and fundamental changes that have taken place in American society.

By this time, the more perceptive and adaptable among my listeners have begun to look thoughtful, if not downright enthusiastic. To these individuals I give reading copies of works by Wister, Ernest Haycox, A. B. Guthrie, Jr., Jack Schaefer, Dorothy Johnson, and other quality writers, and send them on their way. Those who take the time to read just one good Western usually stop being skeptics; and those who can be induced to read more than one often become converts.

Of course, I am careful with the hard-core sneerers and scoffers, those who have the narrowest minds, not to discuss *bad* Westerns, which in truth outnumber the good ones by a wide margin. After all, the whole point of proselytizing is to educate and convert; if I admitted that bad—or what I like to call "alternative" —Westerns not only have flourished like weeds over the past 70-

plus years, but that some of them make Bulwer-Lytton read like a poor man's Shakespeare, I would be reinforcing their know-nothing position rather than my own enlightened one.

So I don't tell them about the alternatives, particularly not the action-oriented type known in the trade as bang-bang horse op-era. And I sure as shootin' don't tell them that I collect and devour the clunkers, the ones so spectacularly awful that they are classics of their kind, with the same zeal and fascination as I do the quality works.

We all have our guilty pleasures; mine is an abiding admiration for alternative fiction in all categories. This passion for the atro-cious, the laughably absurd, led me to write two books about al-ternative crime fiction, GUN IN CHEEK (1982) and SON OF GUN IN CHEEK (1987). And it has now led me, in spite of my ongoing efforts to convince the average reader to rethink his opinion of Westerns, to perpetrate the present volume—a project I undertook only af-ter arming myself with a full set of rationalizations.

First rationalization: A study of bang-bang horse opera may well interest the casual reader in the genre as a whole, giving him pause to reflect that if bad Westerns are such fun, good Westerns must have plenty to offer, too, and therefore leading him to seek out a Wister or a Guthrie or a Johnson.

Second rationalization: The great alternative-Western writers and their works do not deserve to remain trapped and someday lost in obscurity; their peculiar brand of "Joan of Arc romance in glittering armor" should be recognized and lauded for what it is. And who better to be their champion than a True Believer?

Third rationalization: The book will provide a different histori-cal perspective on the many facets of the genre and on the social attitudes it reflects (which are often more pronounced in alterna-tive fiction than in its opposite).

Fourth rationalization: The literary community, like most oth-ers, sometimes takes itself too seriously; critical works tend to be determinedly sober-sided, if not downright pedantic. We can all use a few more chuckles, not to mention a good horselaugh now and then, even if it happens to be at our own expense.

Fifth and final rationalization: The devil made me do it.

It should also be pointed out that the fun I poke in these pages, as was the case with the poked fun in Gun in Cheek and Son of Gun in Cheek, was done with gentle and loving fingers. If it were not for alternative writers and the fruits of their labors, my world would be a far less pleasant place than it is. I bear none of the writers mentioned herein any ill will; on the contrary, I respect them mightily for their accomplishments—fiction that stands well above the mundane, that is every bit as enjoyable in its skewed fashion as any created by those working at the other end of the Western spectrum.

🐎 🐎 🐎 🐎

Before we begin, it seems a good idea to include a glossary of Western slang that the reader will encounter in quotes and references throughout these pages. Colorful vernacular was a staple of the pre-1950 Western story; indeed, in most alternative quarters slang terms and such phonetic spellings as "yuh" for "you," "yore" for "your," and "tuh" for "to" were *de rigeur*. Some yarns are so colloquial in style and content that they are a chore to plow through, containing as they do phrases and euphemisms that even a veteran reader will occasionally find incomprehensible. The following are some of the more common usages. Others of a murkier nature will be defined to the best of my ability as they crop up in the proceedings.

Boss: Big Augur
Cemetery: Boot Hill, skull orchard, underground hotel
Cigarette: brain tablet, quirly
Cook: belly-filler, hotcake herder
Cowboy: brushpopper, buckaroo, cow-nurse, puncher, range warrior, ranny, waddy
Crook/outlaw: buscadero (or busky), hyderphobia skunk, jasper, lobo, noose dodger, owlhooter (or 'hooter), polecat, sidewinder, vinegaroon
Gunfight: gun music, gun-soirée, smoke talk

Gunman: gun-ace, gun-dog, gun-galoot, gunhawk, leather slapper, sixgun smokeroo, slugslammer

Hands/fists: dew-claws, dew-clams, flippers, maulies

Horse: bangtail, bone-pile, bronc, cayuse, crowbait, hayburner, jughead

Liquor: bug juice, coffin varnish, forked lightning, nose paint, tarantula juice, tonsil polish

Preacher: sinbuster, sky-pilot, sky-skipper

Rifle: Ol' Meat-Getter

Saddle: form-fitter, kak, kidney pad, rig, Texas skirt

Sheriff/Marshal: law-dog, star-toter

Sixgun: angel maker, cutter, hogleg (or hawglaig), iron, Judge Colt, lead-pusher, lead-slinger, lead-spitter, pistolian, powder-smoker, slug-slinger, smoke pole, smoke-wagon, smokeroo, talkin' iron

Spurs: gut hooks

Tough guy: he-coon, skookum he-wolf

Young person: younker, button

🐎 🐎 🐎 🐎

Fool or cheat someone: run a whizzer on

Intimidate or frighten: booger

Leave in a hurry: dust, pull your freight

Nervous, antsy: sufferin' from the seam squirrels

Riding or running fast: foggin' it

Shoot dead: salivate

Shrewd, devious: slicker 'n slobbers

"You old bucko!" Fell bellowed like a buffalo bull. "We sure enough figgered they handed you a free grave, or you wouldn't have let this mangy crowbait fog down across our graze like a swarm of locusts. Get up an' heat your kak, younker; we got us a whiz dandy run to turn!" —W. Edmunds Claussen, RUSTLERS OF SLABROCK

1. By the Time I Get to Phoenix; or, Loco Gazabos, Red-Hot Palaver, and Mephistopheles in a Stetson

For the dedicated prospector, the main source of book-length, quality-challenged bang-bang Westerns is the lending-library publishers of the '30s, '40s, and '50s. If such splendid houses as Phoenix Press, Arcadia House, Godwin, and Greenberg had never existed, more than half the number of alternative-class novels would never have been published and many of the tophand authors—Walker A. Tompkins, Archie Joscelyn, Tom Roan, and the many-headed "Jackson Cole," among others—would have remained mired in the pages of the pulp magazines that first spawned them.

In an article published in the WRITER'S 1939 YEAR BOOK, Charles S. Strong, who wrote Westerns as by Chuck Stanley and Northerns as by Charles Stoddard, describes the circulating-library novel as one "designed and planned to fill a longing for light reading in the breasts of those who want to take their books straight, to find them sensational and fast-moving"; and as one "written to entertain and not to air the author's personal viewpoint and outlook on life." He goes on to say that "as a general rule—without casting aspersions—circulating library novels are not the sort of books to be classified as Literature with a capital L, nor are they intended to be [even though] the novels of Charles Dickens and other famous authors were published under an almost identical set-up.... Occasionally they will be reviewed in the current literary journals, but they will not be considered for the Pulitzer prizes. On the other hand they are not as bad as you might think from the above."

Well, yes they are. But since Strong contrived more than a hundred of various types, his point of view is forgivable.

The three main types of lending-library opuses were mysteries, Westerns, and either "sophisticated" (i.e. mildly sexy) or "sweet" romance novels. The books were generally about 60,000 words in length and had bright, sometimes garish, and, in the case of Westerns, often melodramatically pulpy dust jackets. They were "rented or sold to prospective readers in cigar stores, drug stores, book shops, rural post office general stores, railroad stations, gift shops, on trains by American News Company representatives, and sometimes through local book clubs (which are miniature circulating libraries in themselves)." As of 1939 there were an estimated 40,000 lending-library "stands" throughout the country, buying thousands of titles each month and selling them to customers for $2.00 each or renting them at an average fee of 3 cents per day. Cheap fiction for the masses: The novel-form precursor of the paperback original.

By and large, writers of lending-library fiction were also pulp writers who sought extra money by expanding 20,000-, 30,000-, and 40,000-word novelettes and novellas into full-length novels. (Not that the extra cash amounted to a great deal; even by royalty standards of the era, circulating-library publishers paid rock-bottom advances. Phoenix Press, for instance, laid out an average of $200 per book, and unless the author had some name value and/or a shrewd agent, that figure included all subsidiary rights, domestic and foreign.) Some Western fictioneers were novelists first and foremost, writing directly for the LLPs rather than for the pulp markets; Archie Joscelyn, Lee Floren, and Charles Strong were three of the more prolific members of this group. Despite the poor advances and low (if any) royalties, such hardy wordsmiths made their living on volume production and, when they could retain rights, on small sales to the British markets.

The '30s were the boon decade for the LLPs. All of the major houses were born during that time, and even the smaller and

weaker ones thrived for a few years. (There were a handful of purveyors of popular schlock in the '20s—notably Macaulay and
Chelsea House's line of pulp-serial reprints from such Street &
Smith magazines as *Western Story* and *Detective Story;* but as
hokey as some of their titles were, the average Macaulay and Chelsea House book—especially in the Western category—was of a
somewhat higher quality than what the LLPs regularly dished out.)

Arcadia House, Hillman-Curl, and Godwin, which were all part
of the same publishing group, were responsible for scores of oaters
by Tom Curry, Chuck Martin, Johnston McCulley (the creator of
Zorro), Herbert Shappiro, Stuart Adams, Ed Earl Repp, Tom Roan,
Denver Bardwell, and Buck Billings. The William Caslon Company,
during its brief two years of existence (1936–37), specialized in
novels that first appeared in Leo Margulies' Standard Magazines
line of Western-hero pulps—*Texas Rangers, Rio Kid Western,
Masked Rider Western, Range Riders Western*—under such house
names as Jackson Cole. Two years after Caslon's demise, another
short-lived LLP, Gateway Books (1939–42), which was directly af-
filiated with Standard Magazines, published pulp-reprint novels
almost exclusively. Jackson Cole, Buck Billings, and Johnston
McCulley were also in G. H. Watt's stable in the early '30s; Greenberg brought out five early bang-bang Westerns by L. P. Holmes
and others by Nelson Nye and George C. Henderson; Robert
Speller's imprint appears on one novel by A. Leslie (Leslie Scott)
and on Leo Margulies' 1935 gathering of pulp novelettes, WESTERN
THRILLERS.

Dodge Publishing Company's "Two Gun Western" line, edited
by a fairly astute gent with the unlikely name of Critchell Riming-
ton, had perhaps the most consistently readable string of action
gunsmokers between 1937 and 1942. Dodge's leading contributor,
J. E. Grinstead, was a cut above most of his contemporaries, despite having his work appear under such inflammatory titles as
HELLFIRE RANGE and HOT LEAD.

Most of the LLPs were extinct by the end of 1942, having died as
financial failures, been absorbed by other houses, or been killed
off by the paper shortage and government paper restrictions of

World War II. Arcadia House was among the few that survived; its Westerns line lasted well into the '50s. Philadelphia-based Macrae–Smith, which published several titles by Charles H. Snow in the '30s, was another survivor, though they abandoned Westerns until the post-war '40s; they then commenced a new series featuring such luminaries as Walker Tompkins, Louis Trimble, and Roy Manning that lasted until 1956.

The other surviving LLP—the Big Augur of circulating-library publishers—was, of course, Phoenix Press.

Born in 1934, Phoenix began by publishing "sophisticated" love stories under such titles as SPEND THE NIGHT, PUSHOVER, WOMAN HANDLED, and HARD; and Westerns. Its first three horse operas were PURPLE DAWSON, RANCHER by William L. Hawkins, THE SLASH 44 by Al P. Nelson, and THE MEDICO OF PAINTED SPRINGS by James L. Rubel. Phoenix's early success allowed them to begin bringing out Westerns (and mysteries and romances) on a more ambitious scale. Guided first by another unlikely-named gent, Emmanuel Wartels, who was editor-in-chief until 1940, and by Alice Sachs thereafter, Phoenix produced more category novels than any other LLP in the '30s and '40s.

It also produced more alternative classics than *all* the other LLPs combined.

The reign of Phoenix lasted until 1952, when rising printing costs, the burgeoning paperback boom, and the closing of many lending-library outlets forced the company into a merger with its arch-rival, Arcadia House. (The last few Phoenix mysteries and Westerns are strange schizoid mixes; one carries an Arcadia logo on the dust-jacket spine and a Phoenix logo on the book spine, while another carries the Arcadia logo in both places but advertises previous Phoenix titles on the jacket's back cover.)

Alice Sachs was also absorbed in the merger; she assumed command of Arcadia's line of Westerns and (increasingly fewer) mysteries until the early '60s, when the firm underwent another metamorphosis and become Lenox Hill Press. She survived that change, too, and remained Lenox Hill's senior editor, buying Westerns until the line was dropped in 1975 so the firm could expand its more lucrative romance line. At the time of this writing, Lenox Hill is still in business, amazingly enough—the last link to a vanished publishing era—and has resumed the publication of a limited number of Western novels.

For the most part, Phoenix Press books were well packaged. While its mystery and romance dust jackets tended to be two-colored, its Westerns for more than a dozen years were three- and sometimes even four-colored—no doubt because its cover art was either recycled pulp covers or commissioned as originals from pulp-cover artists. It was only in the late '40s, when cost-cutting led to the hiring of less-capable artists and the use of two-color jackets, that the Phoenix Western lost its distinctive look and appeal. Throughout the press's existence, it sanctioned a paper stock of good quality. Equally good were the bindings, though Phoenix's printers, like those of other circulating-library publishers, were prone to using whatever cover stock happened to be on hand, with the result that any one title might have as many as half a dozen variant bindings.

Bang-bang Westerns were Phoenix's number-one seller, so naturally more of these were published over its 18-year life span than either mysteries or romances—an aggregate of some 350 works. Titles ranged from the commonplace to the colorfully pulpy: THE RANGERS OF BLOODY SILVER, THE BANDIT OF BLOODY RUN, THE SAWBONES OF DESOLATE RANGE, HOOT OWL CANYON, BUSH-WHACK BULLETS, GUNSMOKE GALOOT, SLUMGULLION TRAIL, HAIR-TRIGGER HOMBRE, TRAIL TO BANG-UP, LAWDOG OF SKELETON CANYON, CYCLONE OF THE SAGE BRUSH, and WHIZZ FARGO, GUNFIGHTER. The bulk of these sprang from the weedy imaginations of the obscure and forgotten: Tony Adams, Del Morrow, George B. Rodney, Lewis C. Merrill, Al P. Nelson, Clark Frost, Timothy Hayes, Tevis Miller, Robert Claiborne Pitzer, L. W. Emerson, C. L. Edholm, James L. Rubel, T. W. Ford (who also wrote as Abel Shott), and Earle C. Perrenot.

A few notables contributed both original novels and recycled pulp stories early in their careers. Norman A. Fox, who went on to become one of the half-dozen most accomplished writers of traditional Westerns in the '50s and early '60s (his later work was lavishly praised by A. B. Guthrie, Jr., among others), published five Phoenix titles between 1941 and 1943, all pulp-story expansions. Nelson Nye, Western fiction's Jekyll (some of his work is very good) and Hyde (and some is very alternative), was a regular contributor in the late '30s and '40s under his own name and the pseudonyms Clem Colt and Drake C. Denver. Leslie Ernenwein, who would win a Western Writers of America Spur Award for best novel of 1956, dwelt briefly in the Phoenix stable in the early '40s, as did the capable C. William Harrison. Another better than average pulpster, William Hopson, wrote 18 novels for the company, 15 of which were published under his own name and the other three as by John Sims.

And then there were the top guns—four authors whose names (and pen names) appear on more than 20 novels each. Nelson Nye can lay claim to 21. Lee Floren published 23 as by Floren, Brett Austin, Wade Hamilton, Lee Thomas, and Will Watson, and scores more under the Arcadia imprint after the 1952 merger. Charles Stoddard was the second most prolific, with a total of 29 Chuck Stanley yarns unleashed from 1943 to 1952, followed by a nearly equal number of Arcadias throughout the '50s.

In first place, far outdistancing the rest of the field, is the King of Phoenix Westerns, Archie Joscelyn (whose alternative accomplishments we'll examine in the next chapter). Over a span of 15 years, beginning in 1935, Joscelyn published 54 bang-bang sagebrush sagas with the press—23 under his own byline (1935–45), 28 as by Lynn Westland (1936–50), and three as by Tex Holt (1948–50). He also found time to perpetrate two Phoenix mysteries in the late '30s, both of which appeared as by A. A. Archer; and two Phoenix romances in the same period, these under the name Evelyn McKenna.

The plots of Phoenix oaters were standard pulp fare. Cowcountry yarns were the pre-eminent formula; they usually featured lean-hipped, quick-shooting cowboy heroes and stories of cattlemen versus rustlers, nesters, sheepmen, other cattlemen, crooked politicians, crooked mining or railroad interests, or adverse elements such as blizzards and flood-swollen rivers. Other favorites were tales of men wrongfully imprisoned or otherwise sinned-against, or whose friends or relatives were sinned against in some way, who then ride the vengeance trail; cavalry and/or nonmilitary folk in mortal combat with marauding redskins (Indians in Phoenix and other LLP Westerns are always on the warpath, and who can blame them?); and narratives of sheriffs, deputies, Texas Rangers, bounty hunters, railroad or government or range detectives of superhero dimensions (who often sport such stirring nicknames as Deputy Death and Lord Six-Gun) on the trail of outlaw gangs led by an evil supervillain who, like as not, is (a) a megalomaniac after land, money, or some sort of fabulous treasure, (b) elaborately masked, (c) known by such boo-hiss so-briquets as the Border Buzzard or the Riding Devil, and (d) revealed at the end to be a local banker, saloonkeeper, or other prominent citizen.

There were endless variations on these story lines. Here are a few as described briefly by Phoenix's inventive blurb writers, from lists of "New and Forthcoming Phoenix Westerns" that appeared on the backs of dust jackets.

> Trigo Truxton, shady owner of the Bar Nothing, was guilty of crooked gambling devices, blackmail, rustling and even murder until two-fisted Bill Dorne, the straight-shooting sheriff of Spavined Nag and his chief deputy, Brimstone Buck Tranter, rode up. (Clem Colt, THE BAR NOTHING BRAND)

> Lawmen and outlaws alike were hot in pursuit of plucky Steve Larrigan as he rode the hoot-owl trail into Bunchgrass. For he was accused of murdering Abe Valance, a two-faced hombre respected by the law as an upright citizen and by the dread Faceless Riders as their leader. (Archie Joscelyn, COTTONWOOD CANYON)

> Whizz Fargo, a two-gun, fighting waddy, sees three men slain before his eyes—one by Ed Slocum's desperadoes, one by the armed vigilante band known as the Black Sombreros. The third dead man is the father of Caroline Dermody, whose lips are red as gunfire and whose eyes are blue as the desert sky. (George C. Henderson, WHIZZ FARGO, GUNFIGHTER)

The editorial writers waxed even more eloquent in the longer blurbs that graced the front flap of each novel.

> Men called the tough, two-gun marshal of Red Butte Junction "Killer" Kincaid, saying he had frost in his heart and sleet in his veins. This is Kincaid's story. But because it involves the very essence of those halcyon days when the West was a rough-and-tumble frontier, it is also part and parcel of the most glamorous chapter of American history, with all the pungent, devil-be-damned flavor of the era.
>
> Ride with Kincaid into a roaring boom town at end of steel where rowdy, robust men buy their booze and buck the tiger; and listen to guns blast to the tune of pianos playing *Ta-ra-ra-ra Boom De-ay!*" (L. Ernenwein, KINCAID OF RED BUTTE)

✻ ✻ ✻ ✻

These and most other titles in the Phoenix canon are jam-packed with alternative elements, of course. Memorable sentences, passages, characters, plot twists, and gaffes abound. And there are more than a dozen indisputable classics among the 120 or so Phoenix Westerns that I've personally galloped through. In this chapter we'll take a close look at a pair of one-shot Alternative Hall of Fame inductees, each of which was contrived by a relative unknown and each of which, in completely different ways, is a superior example of the art form. In subsequent chapters we'll dissect Hall of Fame gun-blazers by Archie Joscelyn and Walker "Two-Gun" Tompkins and Northern tall tales by Samuel Alexander White—skookum he-wolves, all, in the Phoenix pack who could be counted on to provide chuckles, howls, and nutty surprises in book after book.

Our first inductee, RUSTLERS OF SLABROCK (1946), is what in lesser hands than those of W. Edmunds Claussen would have been a typical cowboys-plagued-by-outlaws yarn. Claussen, however, was a Pennsylvanian who not only grew up reading Wild Westerns but became a fan of such zealous proportions that he and his photographer wife lived in a Western-styled-and-outfitted home that must have startled their neighbors, spent two to three months every summer traveling through the West, and accumulated books and other lore by the carload. As a result of this unbridled passion, the gunsmoke stories he wrote for the pulps and his two Phoenix novels (THE LAWDOG OF SKELETON CANYON was published in 1945) were crammed so full of background material and colloquial lingo that they all but burst at the seams. Claussen was also, at this stage of his career, a clumsy and an adjective- and synonym-haunted writer—other factors that enhance his alternative reputation. (Later, he would hone his skills, learn restraint, and turn out a couple of nonalternative historical adventures published by Dodd, Mead, both of which feature a Colorado River steamboater with the inspired name of Captain Crotch.)

Our old friend, the Phoenix blurb writer, heralds RUSTLERS OF SLABROCK in terms almost as salty as Claussen's:

> It took a throaty-voiced honky-tonk girl at the Crystal Palace to call the turn on Lynn Remole and to point out to the proddy vaquero that quitting the Bar J when it needed him was the act of a belly-crawling sidewinder. So Lynn prepared to back-trail. Instead of gunning for the rustler who had shot down his pal Monty, he would meet trouble on the home range.
>
> Then a stacked card game ended with drawn guns, and Lynn found himself hog-tied by Stud Lasher, the very rustler he sought, and sent travelling on an iron horse.
>
> A ripsnorting yarn of a vengeance-bound pilgrim's adventures in the Slabrock country.

So much for the plot. Leave us at the real delight of this *chef-d'oeuvre*, Claussen's prose.

As noted, he doted on Western slang; he might in fact have been a disciple of the Sultan of Slang, Boothill Chuck Martin, whom we'll meet in Chapter 2. Cowboys, in Slabrock country, are "bull nurses," "cow-tramps," "range warriors," and "waddies," among other things. (And Lynn Remole is the "ace-high ramrod.") Horses are "hayburners," "cowticks," and "snaky nags." Sixguns, of course, are "smokepoles," "cutters," and "powdersmokers." Miners are "gulch rats," tough hombres are "he-coons," outlaws are "demon rod toters" and "sidekicks to a diamondback," a cerebrally challenged individual is a "loco gazabo" or "a thick-skulled short-horn," other men are "jeebows" or "galoots," and all women are "she-birds" or "she-stuff."

Cow-tramps don't get up in the saddle and ride; they "climb in their forks and start foggin'!" or "throw the gut hooks into that cayuse an' get a-hellin'!" Waddies don't have conversations with each other; they hold "red-hot palavers." Bull-nurses don't keep a wary eye out for Indians while riding; they are told to "watch out your stick don't drift on the sign of some scalpin' party cuttin' across your trail." Range warriors don't leave a place; they "cut the breeze" from it. The ace-high ramrod doesn't get angry; he "feels his own gorge risin' near the simmerin' stage." And when he's hit on the head with a smokepole, he wakes up "with a sore pelt between the horns."

A good galoot doesn't suffer from misfortune; he has "bad luck trailin' his rear end." An unattractive she-bird is as "ugly as a Crow wretch with tonsils like a mossy horn." He-coons don't warn each other not to shoot first; they tell their pards "don't uncork a cutter unless the jasper goes for his iron." Nor do they have gunfights with demon rod toters; they "throw lead in their teeth" or "give them a hell-slew of trouble." And they don't tell a sidekick to a diamondback to put up his hands; they "roll out an order" to "stretch for the rafters, killer, if yuh don't want to be salivated!"

Two more examples of Claussen's special brand of red-hot palaver:

> "Stud sneaked up on me with two ugly-looking gunnies while my tail was showing their way. When he asked for a match I dug my paws into my brush jacket and one of his long-haired waddies uncorked an ounce of lead without me even slappin' a six——"
>
> "The ornery, misbegotten polecats——"
>
> "I remember diggin' my head in the sand after I sunfished my saddle. Next thing Lasher, or one of his cow-tramps, dug their heels into my backbone, same as a band of redskins jumping up and down at a medicine show."
>
> "Hot toads, you look like hell! By dammity, what's that white-lookin' stuff hangin' on to your horns?"

"Never mind, Jud. My leg-weary nag's down at Yucca in the feed barn. You run out and saddle me a fresh hayburner. Pick me a fast stepper with plenty of guts."

"*Lace*—or I'm a Apache's brother!" the old plainsman drooled. "Whoever done that wrappin' job sure must like you a heap, younker!"

As the last passage above indicates, Claussen could uncork a mean said substitute when he set his mind to it.

"Go find out yourself," he crackled.

"Hummm," drolled Fell.

"Jiminey cripes, now we got two hayburners here for the same loco galoot," he blatted his bewilderment.

In addition to all the hard riding and fast shooting, RUSTLERS OF SLABROCK has its tender moments, too. Of course, Claussen's idea of romance might not necessarily be yours or mine, as in this exchange between Remole and Monty, his lady love (the first speaker):

"If he stays out of an open grave...I want a crack at that king-pin while the lobos are still ridin' through powdersmoke. You're countin' on me sprawlin' out in your bunkhouse when I get strong enough to hoist my leg over Fiddle, ain't you?"

Remole sobered. "I been having crazy dreams of late. You know I'm not much on she-stuff around a spread, don't you? Well, I been sort of day-dreamin' about you and me...riding circle with our own chuck wagon on my own private range."

"My Gawd, big boy, go on! I'm fair to droolin' at the mouth!"

🐎 🐎 🐎 🐎

Our second one-shot inductee, RANCH OF THE RAVEN (1935), is as different from RUSTLERS OF SLABROCK as a cayuse is from a coyote. For one thing, it is neither a cowboy story nor a vernacular fun-fest. For another, it is a "modern" Western set in Depression-era New Mexico. (Phoenix published a few such bang-bang moderns, just as it published a few Northwest Mounted Police yarns—to give at least the illusion of balance to its Western line, if not to ap-

peal to a broader range of readers.) For a third, RANCH OF THE RA-
VEN is *more* than a Western story; it is also a mystery, a horror tale,
and a sort of desert-country CASTLE OF OTRANTO–style Gothic, all
wrapped up in one mind-boggling package. The sort of book, in
fact, that might have been written by Harry Stephen Keeler, he of
the mad, mad "webwork-plot" mystery novels, if Keeler had decided to try his fine cracked hand at a Western.

Hamilton Craigie, the originator of this screwball masterpiece,
seems to have been a real person; at any rate, eight other Westerns
carrying his byline were published between 1931 and 1953, two of
these by Phoenix Press—NEVADA JONES (1935) and HAIR-TRIGGER
HOMBRE (1946), neither of which I've yet been able to track down.
This one brainchild, however, is more than sufficient to trumpet
his virtuosity and to rescue his name from, as Craigie himself
might have put it in his inimitable style, the swallowing mists, dim
and gray, of that great nonrespecter of the accomplishments of
men, time.

Behold RANCH OF THE RAVEN.

Black Steve Annister, so-called because unlike most Western
heroes he wears a black hat, who is known "in the back blocks of
Wooloomooloof before he had made of that name a by-word in
the honkatonks and the gambling hells from San Francisco
northward to the Wind Rover [sic] country, and beyond it," returns
home from adventuring in the South Seas to find his father, Travis
Annister, a wealthy stockbroker, vanished under mysterious cir-
cumstances. With the aid of a "certain office in a certain side-
street not far distant from the Capitol" (i.e. in Washington, D.C.),
Black Steve—"a bull's bulk of a man [with] the heart of a cougar
and the conscience of a wolf"—follows a three-week-cold trail
that brings him to Dry Bone, New Mexico. Here are just some of
the people he encounters there:

❧ Hamilton Rook, attorney-at-law and owner of Ranch of the Raven, a.k.a. Rancho del Muerte or Ranch of Death, a desert fortress
that looms "as a low, round excrescence like a toad's back beneath
the moon," where ghosts are seen to walk and strange howlings
are heard late at night. Rook, a.k.a. Prince of Plunder, who has "the

heart of a hyena and the conscience of a wolf," is the leader of a secret group of evildoers known by the initials S.S.S. who are responsible for a rash of bank robberies, cattle rustlings, and other nefarious activities. He has a "lean head like a vulture's set upon wide, sloping shoulders [and] the smile of a satyr."

Ɏ Doctor Dominguez, Rook's partner in crime, "half Yaqui and maybe half-Mex," (or is he?), who has hatched a scheme far more insidiously wicked than Rook's S.S.S. He has "a yellow face, a nose like a vulture's, and a smile out of Hell." His nicknames include Jailer of Souls and High Priest of Horror.

Ɏ A South American Jivaro Indian (or is he?) whose visage reminds Black Steve "of a damned soul, unhuman, Satanic…a creature with a face and yet without a face, mewling and meowing like a cat, new come from horrors." His hands are chalklike, malformed, "like the talons of a beast, which in effect they were. The adventurer knew them upon the instant, for, in far off Java, for instance, he had seen those hands, or, rather, the same yet not the same." This specimen also has a sobriquet: Mephistopheles in a Stetson.

Ɏ A legendary and supposedly dead gunslinger named Two-Gun Tone, who perfected "the famous blind draw."

Ɏ Assorted other gunmen with names such as Tucson Charlie Westervelt, Cornudas Jake, Picacho the Horse ("a dark-faced gent with a sand-paper trigger finger"), Two-Gun Guinness (who learned his trade from Two-Gun Tone), and Guinness's partner, the Albino Killer.

Ɏ Poker Hall, Sheriff of Otero County, who has "a face like an Aztec idol's, burned black by the sun."

Ɏ A tough, Prohibition-busting bartender who is known far and wide as "the knight of the bungstarter."

Ɏ A drunken, loco Apache called Mescalero John.

Ɏ A desert rat who appears to be loco and who resembles a scarecrow "with a face like a Hopi mask and skin like a Navajo's."

Y Ciudado Hines, a coot-crazy singing cowboy and foreman of Dumbbell Ranch in Dumbbell Basin.

Y Bull Bogash, ex-leather pusher (prizefighter), whose hands are like stone mauls and who is "a hell-bender, make no mistake!"

Y A girl with red curls, or maybe straight blond hair, who smells like violets, is the niece of Two-Gun Tone, may or may not be named Hattie Marvin, works for Rook as a secretary and house-keeper, may or may not be Rook's mistress, calls herself Little Miss Muffet, and is also a waitress and a lady burglar.

These are some of the things that happen to Black Steve or in which he becomes involved:

Y He is shot at several times, once by a polecat who says "Damn your lights and liver!" and more than once by owlhooters carrying "silenced rifles."

Y He receives all sorts of warning messages, mostly from the red-curled blond, Little Miss Muffet.

Y He is nearly strangled by the Jivaro, whose "face showed like a mask of Huitzilopctil, or of Nacoc Yaotl, god of transmutation, in an Aztec grin." But the Jivaro isn't an Aztec; he's half-Yaqui and maybe half-Mex. Or is he?

Y A violent clash between a sorrel horse and a buck-jumping Model T flivver.

Y The murder of an S.S.S. gang member by a knife flung out of the darkness just as he is about to spill the beans to Black Steve. His last words before he croaks are, "They—they—got me!"

Y A near lynching.

Y A jailbreak.

Y A kidnapping.

Y A "fight to the death" between Black Steve and Bull Bogash, which ends in a sweaty draw with both men still alive.

These are some of the clues Black Steve stumbles across that lead him to the solution of the puzzle:

Y A sponge.

Y A gun containing blank cartridges.

Y A cage at Ranch of the Raven full of howling coyotes.

Y The charred remnant of a blank check bearing the initials TR, the first two letters of his father's first name.

Y A somewhat mangled, gold-toothed dentist's bridge.

And when the solution is finally reached, we learn that:

Y Black Steve is a dick. That is, he is an operative of the U.S. Secret Service, which job was bestowed upon him in the certain office on the certain side street near the Capitol in Washington, D.C.

Y The strangler with the face of a damned soul and the malformed hands like the talons of a beast is none other than Doctor Dominguez in disguise. And he is not a Jivaro Indian, not half-Yaqui and maybe half-Mex, not an Aztec, but actually "a Spaniard, crossed with the Ecuadorian."

Y Hattie Marvin is really Hattie Marvin, Two-Gun Tone's niece, and neither Little Miss Muffet nor Hamilton Rook's mistress. The blond hair is bogus (she donned a wig and also adopted different disguises for obscure investigative reasons) and the red curls are real, which is a good thing because Black Steve never did much care for blondes.

Y Travis Annister has been held captive by the Jailer of Souls, and has "supped full of horrors" as a result, as part of a diabolical scheme in which wealthy men—some of whom are kidnapped (the case of Travis Annister) and some of whom are crooks in search of new identities—are forced to turn over large sums of money and then used as guinea pigs in terrible experiments that either kill them or drive them mad. One of the driven-mad ones, and the only prisoner to escape from Rancho del Muerte, was the putative desert rat with the face like a Hopi mask and the skin of a Navajo, who was formerly a banker named Porter Ide who absconded with his bank's funds. He was also the former owner of the somewhat mangled gold-toothed dentist's bridge.

Ⴤ The High Priest of Horror, a.k.a. Mephistopheles in a Stetson, is a master surgeon who specializes in "forged faces." No, the fiend doesn't practice plastic surgery. He's into something far more devilish than that.

He practices—Dermatology!

"And you've heard of Dermatology...of course. Well...it's been done, in out-of-the-way places, I reckon—practiced to an extent unknown here; we've got something to learn. Well, an anesthetic, and then an operation: new faces for old—forged faces—and the thing was diabolically simple, you see. And the coyotes—that was to cover the—noises, and if anyone should inquire, the beasts had been kept for purposes of experimentation, cross-breeding, you understand. And so when they, the victims, saw themselves in a mirror, sometimes they went loco, for who could prove it? Who would be believed?"

Who, indeed?

All of this ingenious twaddle is told in a prose style that plays hopscotch all over the narrative landscape, from a sort of super-heated Western Gothic—

Grim shadow-shapes, like the bat-like phantasms of some hobgoblin horror, moved before her in a motion-picture of her thoughts. And all at once the plain, the Desert, the sierra, cloud-capped, became a mirage of evil, against which the gun in her holster would be but a toy gun, herself marked down.

Fear, that was not her heritage, came with the sudden thunder of hoofs. From somewhere behind her a gun crashed, flat, without echo, like the plunk of a drum-beat, of a tom-tom, with the swirl and eddy of the riders, as if the ground, sown with dragons' teeth, had vomited them, left, right.

To slangy cowboy patter—

"So long, gents! An' vaya con Dios...nightie-night! Keep goin' straight an' you'll fetch up th' hind side a trouble, less'n it's a mule!"

To violent shades of purple—

> The sun, blazing from high heaven, stippled the meadow with a shimmering iridescence of translucent green. Beneath it the grass seemed drowned in a veil that was like the veil of moving water, with pale fronds like dead-men's-fingers, alive and yet dead.

To comma-choked pseudo-literary exercises, an affliction John D. MacDonald referred to as the "Look, Ma, I'm Writing!" Syndrome—

> Annister, with the gun in his hand, and turned sidewise from the sheriff, rolled and with one hand lighted a cigarette. His fingers appeared to tremble a little, evoking from the sheriff a sardonic gleam, as the paper tube, with a funnel of sparks trailing from it, spurted from Annister's lips, so that, half-turned, he bent to reach for it, fumbling for a moment, so that he was for the moment with his back turned to Hall.

To sinister descriptive passages more at home in a "shudder pulp" horror story than a Phoenix Western—

> A house of silence, broken at times, by a weird wailing as from the Pit; a house of dreams, gray in the moonlight, under the leprous-silvered finger of the moon, brooding now, a grim, gray fortress: the stronghold of hidden horrors—the Rancho of Death.
>
> Dense pines grew about it, so that when the wind wailed among them like the wailing of a lost soul, it met and mingled with an eerie ululation rising as if muffled by many thicknesses of walls, to end, after a while, with a quick shriek and a sudden hush, with, after a moment, the faint echo of a taunting laugh.

But that's not all. Craigie treats his readers to a couple of verses of the cheerful song warbled by Ciudado Hines, the coot-crazy foreman of Dumbbell Ranch:

> "Well, you cowboy shrimps!"
> Old Satan bawled,
> "Yu better be huntin' yore holes!
> F'r I've come up
> Through white-hot rock—
> T' gather in yore souls!"

> Old Satan's grin
> Shore looked like sin—
> His voice rang like a bell:
> "In a lava bed you'll rest yore head,
> Which the same'll be in Hell!"

And now and then a nifty simile:

A gibbous moon, looking like the face of a Mescalero brave drunk on tequila, lighted the dim trail just ahead.

And some rather unique character delineations:

Hines, his brick-red face the color of wet paper, stared, with his jaw fallen, in his set, frozen expression the terrible curiosity that asks and must be answered, no matter what.

Her forehead was not too high, he decided, but it was broad. And her nose. Straight, just as she was, with that indescribable something at the nostrils that told of Race.

And finally, a touch of romance:

Light as the wind against a feather he felt her lips brush him, it might have been the wind, bringing, from the desert spaces, a rare perfume. Sound, and silence, and the beating of a drum. The drum was his heart, was it? Or was it the pound-pound of hoofs?

Neither, I say. What Black Steve may actually have heard was the Jailer of Alternative Classics, the High Priest of Humbug, drumming his heels on the floor in yet another fit of hysterical glee.

"El Lobo hain't got much use fer gents what spy on his doin's. Besides, yo' look like a greaser t'me. Turn around."

A dark tide of blood rose to Dan Chisholm's temples at that. To be compared with a Mexican greaser was an insult that he could scarcely stomach. To be said that he looked like one, well, reason got the better of him and he controlled a sudden desire to fling himself at his accuser.
—Ed Earl Repp, HELL'S HACIENDA

He beckoned to Casey, the bartender, whose head gleamed round and shiny as a Bermuda onion, and who peered jovially out from under a patch where one eye had formerly been.
—Archie Joscelyn, THE SAWBONES OF DESOLATE RANGE

2. Five Aces: Ratt, Roan, Archie, Boot Hill Chuck, and Two-Gun

In any field of endeavor there are individuals whose talent, vision, and accomplishments stand head and shoulders above those of their peers. So, too, in alternative Western fiction. There are several writers such as W. Edmunds Claussen and Hamilton Craigie who were responsible for a single great work, and a few who managed more than one, but only five can be considered true career giants—each for a different reason, and each of whom wrote horse opera unlike anybody else's. This chapter is a tribute to those five aces and their work.

Here, then, Ratt, Roan, Archie, Boot Hill Chuck, and Two-Gun. Up close and personal.

Ed Earl Repp

If I were asked to select the quintessential genre hack writer of this century, the one individual who embodies all the elements of pure unrepentant Grub Street hucksterism, my vote would go to Ed Earl Ratt. I mean, Repp.

In his day, Ed Earl was fairly well known as a supplier of West-

ern and science-fiction pulp—novels as well as short stories—
and as a writer of B-Western movies and serials. From the late '20s
to the early '50s Repp, who first worked as a newspaper reporter,
published some 1,500 pulp yarns and a score of book-length
works, and committed 85 screenplays for Warner Brothers, Columbia, Republic, and RKO (some of which were actually produced, mainly as vehicles in such cowboy series as The Three
Mesquiteers). His bio on the jacket of THE RADIUM POOL, a 1949
collection of three fantasy novelettes, says that Ed Earl "is hailed
as one of the leading magazine fiction writers in the country, specializing in action stories of Western fiction and kindred subjects,"
and that he "still receives fan mail asking for a sequel to 'The Radium Pool' and others of his works."

To merely say that he was a bad writer is to do him something
of an injustice. It would be more appropriate to state that he never
wrote anything by himself—novel, short story, screenplay—that
wasn't bad, including the alleged fan-mail-generating piece of sci-
entifictional nonsense called "The Radium Pool." Some of his *oeuvre* is memorable, to be sure, but only that which appeals to those
of us with an alternative bent.

Repp's peculiar talents are only part of the reason for my nomi-
nation of him as "King Hack." The other part is implicit in the
phrase "by himself" in the previous paragraph. For Ed Earl may
have had 1,500 pulp stories and a score of novels published under
his byline, and his name on 85 screenplays, but he sure as hell
didn't *write* 1,500 stories, 20 novels, and 85 screenplays. Ed Earl,
you see, was something of a nonbenevolent monarchist: He
reigned over a serfdom composed of young, inexperienced, and
hungry writers who did most of his work for him while he sat back
and reaped the rewards.

From 1936 to 1939, one of his serfs was the Western pulpster and
novelist, Frank Bonham. In a 1988 article describing his indentured servitude to the man he referred to as Ed Earl Ratt, Bonham
says that he was "twenty-two years old and prolific as a hamster"
when he answered an advertisement in a Glendale, California,
newspaper: "ESTABLISHED WRITER seeks secretary-collaborator.

You write. I teach and sell. NO FEES." Here is Bonham's account of his first visit to Ed Earl's "home place":

> Ed was a tall, graying man with the air of a million-acre cattleman, and unusually full cheeks that gave him a squirrel-like appearance. He always said howdy as we shook, and when I left it was invariably adios. Years of writing Westerns had seasoned his speech and correspondence with a cowboy saltiness, as a cannery worker might pick up the smell of tuna.
>
> The home place was a ranch-style spread with an elegant bunkhouse, and there were branding irons, spurs, and oxbows all over the living room. We went into a rustic den with at least a thousand pulp magazines on shelves lining the walls, and oil paintings of gunmen getting shot. As Ed sat down to skim my [sample] story, he handed me something of his own to read: a contract setting forth the terms of my indentured service.

The terms were pure Ratt: Bonham was to turn over his entire literary production, and any and all checks would be split 50–50. Meanwhile, Ed Earl would teach young Frank "the tricks of writing" and "encourage" him. Either man could end the partnership at any time, but when that happened all unsold copy would remain Ed Earl's sole property. "It would simplify the bookkeeping, he explained; and anyway all such relationships had to be built on trust. Trust started with my never once seeing one of those checks before it was divided."

Bonham's initial task was to convert scripts Repp had allegedly written for Republic Studios into novelettes, which Repp would then sell to his pulp markets. This didn't work out, for reasons which had to do with Bonham leaking the "twice-told tale" plan to his agent, who also happened to be Ed Earl's agent. So Ratt then encouraged Bonham to come up with fresh fictional material, which he (Repp) would then revise in his own unique style and sell to the pulps under his name.

> Although I didn't know it for some time, he had more ghosts than the Tower of London. Each ghost plotted and wrote his own stories. Ratt then made them smell like the real thing by cramming in pounds of lurid modifiers; and later the checks were divided in two.

Before the partnership ended, I had accumulated the names of four other phantom writers, each of us generating approximately 40,000 words a month which sold in New York for about a cent a word. Through his branding pen passed at least 200,000 words per month, or about $2,000 worth.

Before long, Bonham "knew my Ratty words and phrases by heart [and] could write without flinching 'a bullet tore into his slab-muscled thigh.' All his heroes, early-day Mr. Americas, had slab-muscled thighs. Once a magazine made a typo and it came out 'slab-muscled thing.' Hell of a place to get shot, pardner."

When Bonham began making noises about keeping half of his output to sell under his own name, and then compounded his sin by discussing his working relationship with Repp with an L.A. *Times* columnist, "a curious and frightening thing began to happen. Sales died like dogies at an alkali water-hole. And what sales we managed to achieve were at fire-sale prices." Bonham finally wrote a letter canceling his contract with Repp, and subsequently turned over to him more than 80,000 words of unsold stories— part and parcel of a total indentured output of nearly a million-and-a-half words. Any money Repp later realized from that unsold copy he kept entirely for himself.

King Hack, indeed.

King Ratt.

The following excerpts from novels published as by Repp may or may not have been written by Repp, but he certainly "made them smell like the real thing." The lurid modifiers are there; so are all the other alternative attributes of Ratt-hole–generated fiction.

First, his dazzling descriptive powers, as exemplified in the opening paragraphs of COLT COURIER OF THE RIO.

The Angel of death was poised over the mighty Rio Grande. The somnolence of the Neuces salt grass country was aroused to lethal intensity by its sudden descent, leaving sorrow, shattered dreams and smashed souls in its wake. Blooming Tejano yucca looked upon the carnage, its creamy blossoms seeming to wither at the sight.

The cunning and ruthlessness of the raiders resounded over the salt grass ranges like the clanging waves of a war drum. Texas shuddered at their deadly murderous blows....

By day the sun was a bronze ball in a cobalt sky, sending blistering heat down upon smoldering devastation, mute evidence that the raiders had passed during the night. Carrion birds gorged and hung like specks of black paper in the heavens, owners murdered, their stock driven off [sic]....

Courageous messengers rode dangerous ground for help, only to find the succour they sought ravaged beyond imagination. Ranch-houses and towns alike added their spiralling, smoky headstones against the sky—tell-tale of the latest outrage. The sky was milky with smoke by day, ominous by night. The tawny Chihuahua moon arched across its vault, a blood red ball, giving neither light nor warmth.

Then there was his determinedly phonetic dialogue, which nearly every male character was made to utter.

"Easy with them hawg-laigs, fella," Blanchard warned him. "Jes' outside the windows stands Inky Hawkins, slickest penman in Taixis an' as fast on the belly-shoot as any gent that ever walked. Gut-shootin' you'd be like eatin' fried chicken tuh Inky. An' drillin' yuh right where yore suspenders cross is a feller that's got fourteen notches on his gun-heel—the Big Bend Kid. At the other window an' jes' spraddlin' through is Bull Frayne. Bull's got yore ticket tuh hell in his iron, fella, an' is jes' yearnin' tuh punch it out. Yes siree, I shoulda been a gambler with my hunches, an' I got a hunch right now yuh better git them paws away from yore cutters or enough lead tuh sink yuh tuh China will be slammin' yore way plumb pronto!" (GUN HAWK)

He also had a remarkable ear for the English speech patterns of native Mexicans (or "greasers," as he preferred), for instance those of a *dueña* discussing her charge:

"*El Señor Chubasco* very kind man. My mistress send me for gun. Bristow keeps gun hidden. Mistress want leave this place. No gun. No can leave. You give *Señorita* gun, *Señor*?... She kind like you, *Señor.* You give her gun?" (SUICIDE RANCH)

Repp was never one to allow correct grammar to stand in his

way, especially not when he could sling a lurid modifier, a devastating synonym, and a wicked said substitute:

> The renegade's swart face flamed. Clipping out a curse he grabbed her by the wrist and twisted it cruelly. The Flame but clenched her teeth and made no demonstration, either vocal nor expression [sic].
>
> "Yo're lyin'!" charged the cruelster. (COLT COURIER OF THE RIO)

> "Bristo!" he cracked out through parched lips.
>
> The renegade peered through the dust of conflict and his crazed eyes lit with fury. "You!" he swore luridly.
>
> "For the Flame!" hissed Jim, and let go with both guns. (COLT COURIER OF THE RIO)

Colorful action writing was another of his alternative long suits, in the following case quite literally colorful:

> "I'll let you up, you dirty greaser!" snarled Dan furiously. "I'll send you to hell!"
>
> The savage animal instinct that lies in the depths of all men seized him suddenly with all its beastly fury.
>
> His fingers bit into Contreras' brown throat like talons. Pedro's face went white beneath his blood-smears, then green. Suddenly it became blue with strangulation.
>
> Contreras' tongue projected itself suddenly from between colorless lips. It was black with strangulation. (HELL'S HACIENDA)

And what of Repp's Western plots? Well, this is the sum of his 1936 novel GUN HAWK, as described by his British publisher, Wright & Brown, in its jacket blurb:

> Cowskin was being bled to the bone by the reign of terror of The Devil's Disciples, a gang of self-installed vigilantes. Ranches were stolen, herds ravaged and men lynched wholesale by this unholy crowd. And then Steve Hale came home from California to find they had lynched his father, Bronco Hale, and Johnny, his younger brother. Returning, he found the bodies swaying dismally in the storm that swept wildly over the valleys.
>
> Then Steve, known as The Gun Hawk, rides the trail of vengeance, swearing to kill the father of the girl he loves, as one of the Disciples. How does Steve get around the killing of his sweetheart's

father? Does he carry out his oath of vengeance or does he let him live out of love for Terry Holcomb?

The answer to the last question above is, "Of course." If there's one thing a clever Ratt knows, it's how to bring home the cheese.

Tom Roan

Tom Roan was like a character in one of his hell-roarin' stories: hero and villain all wrapped up in one lusty, violent, brave, foolish, muleheaded, bigoted, gaudy, and outrageous package.

Born in a lawless hill-country section of Alabama, where the towns purportedly had such names as Slick Lizard Ridge and Bloody Beat 22, Roan ran away from his home town of Attalla at age 13 to seek his fortune. Four years later he took a job no one else wanted: marshal of a Wyoming community he claimed was "the toughest town next door to hell," where the statement was made that "a man ain't a man until he's killed at least once, and a marshal never until he has three notches on his guns." But in those days wanderlust ruled him and he never spent more than a short time in any one place; after six months he moved on to such other manly pursuits as bronc-buster, horse-trader, circus rider, railroad special agent, and U.S. Army soldier and scout in such far-flung locales as Hawaii and the Orient.

According to friend and fellow Western writer Frank C. Robertson, in a memorial published in the Western Writers of America *Roundup* after Roan's death in 1958, Roan was a bitter foe of union labor and worked as a "company detective," i.e. union-buster, in San Francisco—probably for a railroad or a rail-related business. From there he went into law enforcement in Idaho, where he was a deputy sheriff of Bannack County. Although he hated the Volstead act as much as he hated unions, he was responsible for arresting more bootleggers in Idaho and Utah during Prohibition than any other law officer.

Roan also engaged in more than one Old West–style shootout. In one he wounded a notorious outlaw and murderer who was subsequently executed at the Washington state prison in Walla Walla. He alludes to another gunfight in the dedication to one of his novels, GAMBLERS IN GUNSMOKE, which reads in part: "To Coe Hatch—my loyal, long-time friend...and to the memory of two grand old .44's thundering in the bitter-cold moonlight; to three hired killers in ambush spilling dying blood on the snow—and the emerald-green eyes in the beautiful face of a lying Irish wench sometimes called Boots."

Roan began pounding a typewriter in 1919, as an avocation, and grew so successful at it that he eventually gave up law enforcement and turned to free-lance fiction writing as a full-time profession. His byline appeared on hundreds of Western, adventure, and crime stories in a wide range of pulp magazines, including *Western Story, Dime Western, Adventure, Blue Book, Detective Fiction Weekly,* and *Detective Tales,* and on more than a dozen novels (among them the 1936 alternative Yellow Peril mystery classic, THE DRAGON STRIKES BACK, about which see GUN IN CHEEK). Much of his work reflects his pet hates, which Frank C. Robertson listed as including Communists, Northern Negroes, union leaders, foreigners (especially Orientals), the New Deal, and the Eisenhower administration.

Roan, in fact, seems not to have liked much of anything or anybody, except for his second wife and daughter, and animals in general and dogs in particular. His best stories—a few of which, published in *Blue Book* in the '50s, actually border on the sentimental—have four-footed rather than two-footed protagonists.

His Westerns are as emotionally charged and feverishly melodramatic as his life. No one created more offbeat and often unheroic heroes; no one invented nastier villains and then disposed of them with greater savagery and relish. No one wrote more sensational blood-and-thunder scenes, or made pitched gun battles seem so cosmic, as if they were miniature Armageddons. Everything in a Roan Western has a larger-than-life feel, grandiose on the one hand and ridiculous on the other. He was the pulp-writer equivalent of a slightly cracked hellfire-and-brimstone preacher, spewing forth dire warnings and wild imaginings and calling down the mighty wrath of God on the wicked and unrepentant.

This is how Good triumphs over Evil in two of his books:

Peacemakers filled his hands as if explosions threw them there. "You'll take 'em only with me smokin' 'em!"

It was like a jump, a flash from slow movement into all-shattering noise and spouting of instantaneous red hell erupting. Roar on roar filled the room, appearing to bulge the windows and start the drapes whipping, blowing, ballooning and bellying.

Down on the floor was a bouncing, rolling, tossing thing turned to lightning movement and fury. He was all fire and smoke....

The wildest, craziest thing of it all was on the stairs. It was the red-faced bull up there who called himself Galliger O'Brien. Dancing, crying, jabbing and poking, he was trying to reload a shotgun with Dude Marlin spinning like a fighting bumblebee on the floor.

A Peacemaker seemed to jump upward from the floor. From its hot muzzle tore a long yard of brilliant yellow flame. Two red hands dropped a shotgun, and Galliger O'Brien was pitching face-forward on the stairs and suddenly coming down, bouncing, rolling, shotgun bounding along like a rimless spinning wheel beside him. As if trying to burst his belly open he landed flat at the foot of the steps. (GAMBLERS IN GUNSMOKE)

It was murder, all the way around the muddy circle, but murder was the order of the day this Wyoming morning in the valley.... Thunder and damnation in a yard of flames and smoke from the left that might have come from a blunderbuss.... Voices sobbing, gasping, men sinking, men falling back...leaping, ducking, side-stepping devil dancers, going through their paces in the unmerry hell of a gunfight.

It was over as quickly as it had started. A gunfight never lasts long in such close quarters. It had been like a house suddenly falling, like a bridge coming apart at both ends and in the middle at the same time, the wreckage flying and coming down in every direction. (RAWHIDERS)

Roan's dialogue had a similar flamboyance and crack-of-doom harshness:

"Eat 'em up alive, yuh punkin' heads!" Old Bow and Arrow Hank's voice lifted like a squalling wildcat above the din. "Wrop their ankles 'round their jawbones! Surrender, would yuh? Shore!" *Boom!–boom!* "Smack-dab betwix the eyeballs! Hold yore fire, Gourd Head! Yuh good-for-nothing rattle-brain.... Jes block-heads! What else could yuh 'spect of 'em? Raised like goats, an' I believe the bell-wether of the breed was a ram!" (GUN LORD OF SILVER RIVER)

But it was his characters that really set his work apart from that of his peers, alternatively and otherwise. Novels and stories alike bulge with a kaleidoscopically absurd array of protagonists, antagonists, combinations of the two, and secondary characters. For instance: Fate Landlock, tough young sheriff of Silver River Bend, Wyoming (he considers himself "cholera morbus, hydrophobia, a ring-tailed catawampus"), who runs afoul of a couple of high-toned dudes breeding sheep on the old Billy B. Damn Place at one end of his valley, and of old Ma Bushwacker, her husband Bow and Arrow Hank Bushwacker, and her son Gourd Head Bushwacker, a bunch "so mean they hated themselves" who are running great herds of cattle through Devil's Ladder Gorge at the other end of the valley; and unto the bargain he (Fate Landlock) must contend with assorted good- and bad-intentioned sorts named Scatter-brain Jackson, Jasper Fuddy, Hard Hammer Hatfield, Madhat Charley Yawberry, Boss Badger, and Hood Arnold, the Lynx of the Pecos (GUN LORD OF SILVER RIVER).

For two more instances: Parson Dave Gambler, "the Psalm-Singing Bandit," and his son, the Overland Kid ("born on the gun-trail from an outlaw mother"), who set out to hold up a train and steal a mine payroll headed for McDood's Bank in Lost Spur, and instead end up bringing a much nastier group of owlhooters, Shark Finn of Texas and his band of "gun-pups," to justice in a wild shootout inside the Texas Cowboy Saloon ("Reformation of the Two-Man Wild Bunch," *Dime Western*); and Anvil Lord, known as the Gun Lord of the Pecos and the Rio Grande, who with a son called Devil Lord, a stepson named Brill Wilde, and a murderous, one-eyed old horsethief sporting the elegant handle of Don Juan Leon de Casa Grande, travels in wagons with "long black stripes down the backbones of their tops" that are drawn by oxen and driven by "bearded bullwhackers chewing stout tobacco," and who starts an all-out range war when he and his motley crew drive 6,000 head of Longhorn cattle over the rim of Music Mesa and then across peaceful Golden Valley "like blood spilling down the green grass" (RAWHIDERS).

Roan's fictional people weren't just bombastic and bizarre in name and action; they *looked* that way, too.

> An expression of hunger and weariness had settled in Old Heck Kilada's face. Squashed under the broken brim of an old black Stetson, it was shorn and Mongolic, about the color of a sunburned strawberry and long in need of a stout scrubbing with soap and water. A knife-scar marred it, running like a run left by a hot wire from above the left eye and down across the bridge of his bulbous, pock-marked nose to the lobe of his right ear. A week's stubble of reddish beard, as sunburned as his face and sprinkled with gray, clouded his bulldoggish jaws, the stubborn chin and the wide, loose lips. His eyes were brown and almost piggish, shaded by tangled lumps of brows and forever squinting. His hair was thin on the top of his head and as coarse as a bull's tail. "Store-bought" teeth filled his mouth and aggravated an already aggravated disposition that was as quick as gun-powder and as dangerous as dynamite. (SMOKY RIVER)

> "Look at 'im! Longest legs I ever saw on anything except a grandaddy spider, neck on 'im like a giraffe, head like a lop-sided gourd, an' a face like a Comanche tomahawk! Ever'time I look at 'im I wonder what kind of a varmint it was that scared his mammy just 'fore he was born. So deef he can't hear a double-barreled shotgun go off at the back of his head. An' acts so dumb in both brain an' tongue, you'll think he's got no more sense than a sagebrush gopher."

> Legs Smith was coming to a halt in front of the porch...longer and thinner than he had looked from the distance. A battered old gray hat was jammed on the back of his head. His face was as drawn and shrunken as that of a long-dry corpse, the eyes those of a ghost, twinkling pale lights deep in their sockets. He threw back his head and made a noise that was probably intended for laughter, but it was more like the shuddering cry of an owl. (GAMBLERS IN GUNSMOKE)

Vicious killers, you think? Not at all. Both Old Heck Kilada and Legs Smith are more or less typical Roan heroes!

Frank C. Robertson closed his *Roundup* memorial by opining

that there will never be another man or another writer like Tom Roan. To which I say, "Amen."

Archie Joscelyn

Remarkably prolific over a career that spanned nearly a half a century, Archie Joscelyn was responsible not only for 54 Phoenix Press Westerns but for another 49 oaters under his own name and more than a hundred others as by Lynn Westland, Al Cody, and Tex Holt. Add to that 200-plus total a dozen mystery, romance, and juvenile novels and a hundred or so pulp stories, and you have a career fictional output of around 15 million words. Ninety-five percent of his novels were written for lending-library publishers — Avalon, Lenox Hill, and Bouregy, in addition to Phoenix and Arcadia House. His only fling with a respected trade publisher was in the late '40s and early '50s, when he published nine Al Cody–bylined action Westerns with Dodd, Mead.

A native Montanan, Joscelyn was once quoted as saying, "I chased cayuses from the backs of others; smelt burning hair from the branding iron and rode all day behind half-tamed dogies with the barbed wire steadily encroaching. And then I tried to put some of it down on paper — to catch something of that lingering whisper out of the past, a bit of the remaining glory of a golden age."

To a certain extent, he succeeded in his aim. As a born-and-bred Westerner he was able to convey a more or less authentic feel for the Old West and the people who inhabited it. He had a sense of history, and his research was good enough to enable him to include background detail of some interest (such as early railroad track-laying methods in the 1942 Lynn Westland bang-banger, SHOOTIN' IRON). His narrative style was generally a notch above that of his circulating-library peers: adequate descriptive powers, dialogue that wasn't overloaded with colloquialisms and phonetic spellings. And his characters tended not to be shaped wholly out of cardboard stock.

Nor was he content to write nothing more than cow-country yarns with minor variations. He also composed blood-and-thunder novels with mining, fur-trading, railroading, and freighting

backgrounds; novels set on riverboats, in deserts and on mountains, at isolated frontier outposts; novels whose protagonists are
doctors, clerks, gamblers, rodeo performers, mountain men.

If his multitude of Westerns had been limited to such relatively
positive components, Joscelyn would have been just another pur-
veyor of pulp and thus of little alternative interest. Fortunately, he
had two other qualities that crop up time and again in his stories.
One is a penchant for the manufacture of unintentionally funny
passages of narrative and dialogue—glittering nuggets among all
the semi-polished prose stones, as if every now and then a cell or
two in his febrile brain short-circuited in wondrously alchemic
ways. One such nugget serves as this chapter's epigraph. Here is a
sampling of others:

Expensive jewelry flashed from his fingers and stick-pin. (PRENTISS
OF THE BOX 8, Lynn Westland)

Overhead, a pale moon flitted among a ghostly mist of fainting
stars. (THE SAWBONES OF DESOLATE RANGE)

Somewhere a coyote howled in a strange medley of tongues.
(PRENTISS OF THE BOX 8)

For a moment he glared, lips drawn back from nervous teeth.
(HANGMAN'S COULEE, Al Cody)

Some sixth sense, which he rather preferred to call a hunch,
warned him that there was a gentleman of dubious color buried
somewhere in this wood pile which they wanted him to saw. (TRAIL
TO MONTANA, Lynn Westland)

Yet all this, Scotty knew, was illusory, a transitory thing of imper-
manence. (KING OF THE RODEO, Lynn Westland)

The man was a typical cattleman—middle-aged, saddle-filling, but
not fat, with a brown mustache with adventurous tendencies below
slightly graying hair. (PRENTISS OF THE BOX 8)

"Since I see a ray of light ahead for both of us, I'll be as shy as a colt
watchin' a piece of paper." (THE RANGE OF NO RETURN, Lynn Westland)

There were low, broken hills thereabouts, with frequent patches of
brush and some scattering trees. (TRAIL TO MONTANA)

> She appeared to be about eighteen [and] her eyes…were brown—
> almost but not quite black—while her skin, by contrast, was fair as
> new-fallen snow on an old fence rail. (TRAIL TO MONTANA)

Now and then Archie could come up with an alternative narrative hook, too, as in these opening paragraphs of three Phoenix Press sagas:

> The freight train swung around a curve and slowed for the water
> tank and the town behind, sighing softly from a hard run as it
> gulped down a drink. (PRENTISS OF THE BOX 8)

> "You weel elevate the hands, Msieu—high above the head, so, like
> you were reaching for the very stars themselves. Stars that, so very
> far away, may yet be so easy to grasp, yes." (GUNS OF LOST VALLEY)

> The prairie had about run its course here. To the east and south it
> spread, weary mile on mile, as flat and unending and monotonous
> as a yellow hound dog scratching at fleas. (SHOOTIN' IRON)

Joscelyn's other alternative attribute was a knack for devising plot twists of dazzlingly wacky proportions. Inasmuch as the LLP Western formula called for at least half a dozen action scenes per book, he was challenged continually to invent new and different methods of getting his heroes into and then out of dire predicaments. Shootouts, knife fights, and fisticuffs were all well and good, but there are only so many variations that can be rung in on each of them. Blowing up people and things—buildings, dams, mountains—with dynamite served him well, but this ploy, too, has its limits.

So he also pitted his fighting men against animal and natural menaces in addition to human ones. Wolves, dogs, bears, and stampeding cattle were his favorite beast hazards. Mother Nature provided fast-current rivers and swollen creeks and mountain streams, into which protagonists either fell or were thrown; violent storms, blizzards being the preferred type; landslides, mudslides, avalanches; raging floods, forest fires, and yes, even earthquakes. But he wasn't content to utilize such perils in standard ways. His fecund imagination produced uncannily original variations, some of which show the stamp of genius.

Consider this sequence in a 1939 Lynn Westland classic, THE
RANGE OF NO RETURN: Smoke Marlow, a fearless gunslamming
buckaroo so named because he "made men watch his smoke
when he moved," and a small band of other rannies are about to
be fried bacon-crisp in a fire set by a ruthless bunch of fugitives on
Cayuse Mountain. There seems to be no way to escape the raging
inferno; hell-hot flames surround the men on all sides. A wooden
flume built on poles nearly a hundred feet off the ground runs up
the side of the mountain, "built huge for irrigation purposes," but
it's bound to burn up, too, in the on-rushing flames...or is it? No!
For the flume has been constructed of wood fortuitously painted
with a fire-retardant that not even a forest fire advancing in "a mad
orgy of consumption" can destroy.

So Smoke and the boys climb up into the flume, which is filled
with a few inches of water. But wait! One of the outlaws, safe above
the blaze, witnesses the climb and opens the sluice gate at the top
of the flume, allowing a flood of icy water to rush downward. The
good guys are sure to be drowned, or swept off and plunged to the
now-burning terrain below...or are they? No! Smoke spies an ax
that has been fastened to the inside of the chute in the event water
should freeze during the winter and the ice need to be chopped up
(?). But he can't climb up the steep-slanted flume to where the ax
is because of the rushing water and the slippery footing...or can
he? Yes!

First, though, he locates a convenient knothole, through which
he lowers and ties his lariat, which he happens to have had looped
over his shoulder all along; this allows the others to climb out of
the water and over the side of the flume, then to hang from the
rope above where "the fire raged like an inferno" while he goes after the ax. This feat he accomplishes by taking his knife in one
hand and a pard's knife in the other and alternately digging their
blades into the chute's sides, thus pulling himself up to where the
ax is attached. Then he slams the ax blade into the wall and uses
that to pull himself up atop the flume, which he straddles with his
great muscular legs to give himself leverage. And then he chops
holes in the bottom and sides of the flume, through which much

of the water gushes out. This not only saves his and his comrades' lives, but the water "spraying a section nearly a hundred feet in diameter as it struck and running in a stream on down the hill" puts out the fire and enables the men to climb down the rope to complete safety.

Whew!

Or how about these inspired bits of business in a Joscelyn epic, GUNS OF LOST VALLEY (1940): Rimrock Vance, on the trail of an ancient hidden treasure reputedly guarded by the mysterious and legendary Iron Men in the nightmare-haunted canyons of Lost Valley, is taken prisoner by his nemesis, Sheriff Blaze Barnigan, "the softest-spoken scoundrel who ever slit a throat." The capture happens shortly after Vance and his lady love, Laurene, locate the hidden treasure in a cavern behind a waterfall. (Joscelyn and his alternative peers purely loved caverns, caves, tunnels, and subterranean grottos, especially when access to same was hidden behind a waterfall. A good percentage of the action in every third LLP oater takes place underground.)

Where were we? Oh yes, Rimrock Vance and his lady love, Laurene, have just located the hidden treasure and not incidentally identified the legendary Iron Men, whose skeletal remains they have also found in the cavern, as a small party of Spanish conquistadors who got separated from Cortez's main army and wandered off in search of the Seven Golden Cities of Cibola. Enter Blaze Barnigan and his gang, a bunch of superstitious Indians led by a chief named Dragging Claw. Rimrock is spirited away to a nearby cabin, tied hand and foot, and placed under guard; Laurene, meanwhile, is in the clutches of Blaze Barnigan and presumably about to suffer the usual fate worse than death. Her only hope is Vance, who must save her at all costs.

First order of business: Get free of his bonds. But how? On the floor of the cabin he notices a bearskin rug, complete with huge bear paws, and on the bear paws are long, sharp claws; Rimrock snags one of his rope knots on a claw and deftly works it loose. Then, free at last, he dons the heavy bearskin, entices the guard outside to enter the cabin, and then "crashed a huge paw down on his head." After which he charges toward a second Indian warming himself at a bonfire: "There was a startled, incredulous look on the guard's face at the sight of the bear coming at him. Rimrock threw the heavy skin, enveloping him like a blanket, sending him sprawling." And off he races.

Our hero manages to reach the cavern behind the waterfall without further incident, despite the fact that Dragging Claw's braves are in hot pursuit, and slips inside the vault where the Iron Men's bones are seated around a stone table. Blaze Barnigan is somewhere nearby, but Vance can't fight his nemesis and save Laurene without some kind of weapon. Ah, how about one of the Iron Men's spears? Good, but not quite good enough: "Spears against bullets was nothing to chuckle about."

Another brainstorm strikes almost immediately: He'll put on one of the conquistador skeleton's suit of armor! "He had to work fast, but his experience in studying old armor would not be amiss now. Being a Rhodes scholar might be worthwhile, after all. [Oh, I didn't mention that Rimrock Vance was a Rhodes scholar? Well, he is.] He had taken suits of armor apart and assembled them times enough, had worn two or three on occasion at masquerades." And so, encased in the rusty iron suit, "peering out from between the slit" in the heavy casque over his head, Rimrock clanks and creaks deeper into the cavern, where he finally encounters Blaze Barnigan about to put the moves on the lovely Laurene.

Vance attempts to skewer the outlaw lawman with his spear, "but a spear from a gauntleted hand, with his whole body hampered by the unaccustomed weight of the armor, was far from being the same thing as tossing a javelin at an athletic meet, as he had done years before." A terrible battle ensues, with Blaze blazing away at Rimrock with a pistol and Rimrock trying to crush Barnigan's head like an eggshell with his mailed fist. It is at that moment, with the Indians closing in on one side and Blaze Barnigan about to get the upper hand in the fight because of the cumbersome suit of armor restricting Rimrock's movements, when another earthquake suddenly hits with tremendous force. (Oh, I didn't mention that earth tremors have been plaguing Lost Valley?

Well, they have.)

This is a Big One: "It smote Rimrock like a giant hand, the ground seemed to twist and heave under him, the roar was a thunder like a freight train crossing an iron trestle at high speed." He is knocked off his weighted feet and pelted with falling rock, but the "iron tuxedo," which had been "cramping his style when he tried to fight," saves him from serious injury. He clanks and rattles his way to Laurene, who is also unhurt but who confides sobbingly that she's "terrified—just plain scared!" Soon they manage to make their way to freedom (Rimrock still in his iron tuxedo), leaving behind Blaze Barnigan, Dragging Claw and his braves, the skeletons of the Iron Men, and the lost treasure that may or may not have come from the Seven Golden Cities of Cibola, all of which have been buried forever beneath tons of rock.

Double whew!

See what I mean about genius?

Charles M. "Chuck" Martin

In the '20s and '30s Boot Hill Chuck Martin was one of pulp fiction's legendary million-words-a-year crankers. He was also cut from the same cloth as Tom Roan: a genuine character.

Another Westerner born and bred, Martin had first-hand knowledge of cowboy and ranching life, having worked on two huge California cattle ranches in the early years of the century. He claimed to have fought with Pancho Villa in Mexico, and to have known Wyatt Earp and the Daltons. After the fashion of his fictional heroes, he was a brawling, hard-drinking individualist: salty, opinionated, violently patriotic. He carried on feuds with editors and other writers, and worked so hard at fictioneering, writing two weekly newspaper columns (one for the *Brewery Gulch Gazette*), and at various other pursuits (horse training, pistol shooting, oil painting, raising flowering cacti) that he suffered at least one nervous breakdown.

He believed passionately in the stories he wrote, so much so that for him his fictional creations were real people and therefore entitled to the same privileges and courtesies. On the back-forty of his Oceanside ranch he constructed a small private graveyard, complete with handmade tombstones, which he called Boot Hill Cemetery and in which he solemnly "buried" the characters he killed off in his Westerns.

Martin began writing for the pulps—in particular, for such Clayton and Hersey magazines as *Cowboy Stories, Ace-High Western,* and *Ranch Romances*—in the years following the end of World War I, and for more than two decades he was one of the half-dozen most prolific producers of flaming-lead-and-pounding-hoofs-on-every-page horse opera. He boasted of an output, on good days, of 10,000 words at a single sitting. In 1929 he earned upwards of $1,500 per month for his pulp work—a princely sum in those days. By 1941 he had published 850 magazine stories by his own count, mostly novellas and novelettes, and 29 full-length novels under his own name and the pseudonym Clay Starr.

Few writers can keep up such a white-hot production pace indefinitely; Boot Hill Chuck was no exception. "The million-word-a-year man," he once wrote, "was sired by low rates, and killed off by his own exertion." Changing market requirements, and his inability to adapt to them, also contributed to his decline from a big-name Western pulpster to one who, for the last decade and a half of his career, only sporadically wrote and sold Western fiction. Virtually no short stories and a dozen or so novels appeared under his byline between 1944 and his death in 1954. (Four other novels were published posthumously.)

Series characters were the stock-in-trade of the Western wordsmith, and Martin created his fair share. Notable among them were an aging gunslammer and Wells Fargo troubleshooter, Alamo Bowie, who is "fast with his tools" and "carries the salty tang of powdersmoke in his blood," and who appears in numerous pulp stories and such novels as Law for Tombstone (1937) and Gun Law (1938); peripatetic cowboys Roaming Reynolds and Texas Joe, star performers in a string of adventures, including Deuce of Diamonds and Double or Nothing, both published in 1938; and "Gospel" Cummings, a drunken, Bible-spouting gun artist and self-appointed caretaker of Boot Hill (not unlike his creator), who casts a giant shadow in THE LOBO BREED (1951), BOOT HILL GOSPEL (1951), and GUNSMOKE BONANZA (1952).

Cummings is easily Martin's most interesting hero. He is described in BOOT HILL GOSPEL as "a man with a dual personality. The good man of his nature lived on the left side, where his heart was. In the left tail of his coat, he carried a well-thumbed copy of Holy Writ. The bad man of his nature lived on the right side. It was there he carried a balanced Colt .45 six-shooter [and] a quarter of Three Daisies Whiskey, the token of his besetting sin....."

But it is Boot Hill Chuck's prose that is the token of his besetting alternativeness. It has tremendous energy and drive, of the sort that can be created only by True Believers, but it is so colloquial and so determinedly, unrelentingly Western that it approaches self-parody. His characters don't look for trouble; they "kick up hot ashes in the devil's coal pile." They don't draw sixguns; they "skin the leather off the old smoke-pole." They don't eat; they "iron the wrinkles from their bellies." They don't drink liquor; they "cut the trail dust from their windpipes with a shot o' coffin varnish." He was the first and true Sultan of Slang, the Big Augur whose style and vision pale the copycat efforts of the likes of W. Edmunds Claussen into insignificance.

The dialogue in a Boot Hill Chuck story is an experience and an education. Savor these passages in all their colloquial, lyrical, and alternative purity:

> "Elevate, you mangy old wart-hog!" a twangy voice barked from the brush. "I shot that Bisley Colt from your filly's hand, and never broke the skin. With you it will be different, you long-jointed old pelican. Drop your Winchester and sky them dew-claws before I do you a mean-ness!" (TWO-GUN FURY)

> "They got Bobbie," Zander groaned. "Them two stepped in before me and Bobbie knew what for, and Ramrod McCall had Bobbie before I could slap for my hawg-laig. I see Red Frasier make a swipe to buffalo me with his gun-barrel, and the next thing I knowed I was laying there hog-tied like a leppy...."
>
> "I'll kill him with my bare maulies," Manny Lassiter growled savagely. (DEUCE OF DIAMONDS)

"I'll pay you what you gave for that land or kill you, one. My stock is grazing on this range, and I don't aim to move 'em. You heard my wau-wau!" (Two-Gun Fury)

"Elevate, you old sinbuster. Get them dew-claws ear-high before I bust a cap!" (Gunsmoke Bonanza)

"Sky them dew-claws, the lot of you! First man that reaches for an iron is due to kick hot ashes in hell!" (Deuce of Diamonds)

"Better put a clothespin on your nose. That big poke stinks like a nest of wood pussies after a long cold winter." (Two-Gun Fury)

Some of Martin's slang expressions, as the foregoing passages demonstrate, are of the arcane sort. "Wau-wau," in case you're wondering, is not Western baby talk for dog; it means "war talk." "Poke" is an abbreviation of "cowpoke," another euphemism for cowboy. And "wood pussies," of course, are skunks. I'm not quite sure what a "leppy" is. Nor am I quite sure what Boot Hill Chuck was trying to say when he wrote the following line:

Roaming Reynolds glared and caught up his whang. (Deuce of Diamonds)

He had a fondness for said substitutes, too, including such clever ones as "creaked," as in "he creaked brokenly." Another fondness was adverbs, especially as modifiers for his said substitutes. Curiously, he sometimes put the said substitute together with an adverb meaning the same thing, thus creating some interesting redundancies. All of the following are from Deuce of Diamonds:

"I dunno," Reynolds drawled slowly.

"Any time, you busted flush," he sneered nastily.

"You bought chips in a closed game, feller," he rasped hoarsely.

"Let him have it now, Shorty," the big puncher snarled viciously.

"I'll back you," Manny Lester growled huskily.

"I knew it," he murmured softly.

"I found two dead men in my front room," Tyson grated harshly.

Metaphor mixing was another of his alternative long suits:

Like a flashing reflection, the Deuce of Diamonds ramrod made his strike like a hawk in full flight.

As was an occasional brilliant, if unintentional, pun:

The undertaker did not remove his eyes from the tall gun-fighter. "My business is to bury the dead," he answered gravely. (DEUCE OF DIAMONDS)

Boot Hill Chuck, like Tom Roan, was an Original. We won't see his like again, either.

Walker A. "Two-Gun" Tompkins

In a 1979 letter to a fanzine, Walker Tompkins wrote that he "ground out millions of words of Western pulp between 1931, when Street & Smith bought my first novelette for *Wild West Weekly,* until the mid-fifties when the genre faded before the competition of old debbil television." Using his own name and a plethora of pseudonyms and house names, he was a regular contributor to *Wild West Weekly, Ranch Romances,* and particularly Leo Margulies' Standard Magazine group, for which he wrote scores of lead novellas for such Western hero pulps as *The Rio Kid Western* and *Masked Rider Western.* He was so fecund, and maintained such a white-hot production pace (he could type upwards of 100 words a minute on a manual typewriter, and religiously wrote 6,000 words each day, five days a week, in an old house trailer he used for an office), his fellow pulpsters honored him with the "Two-Gun" sobriquet.

He worked even while on one of his frequent trips to various U.S. and foreign locales. In his 1979 fanzine letter he claimed to have once "carried my Corona portable to the top of the Pyramid of Cheops and spent a day knocking out a novelette which I mailed to my editor in New York. It was published, as I recall, under the title of 'Tombstone Calaboose,' no doubt the only literary masterpiece ever composed in such an exotic setting." A good anecdote, this, but probably apocryphal. Back in 1939, in a *Writer's*

Digest article called "Plotting the Pulp Western Story," he mentions having gotten only the basic idea for "Tombstone Calaboose" atop the Great Pyramid, which he jotted down in his notebook as "Write a cowboy story based on theme that a man can't take riches with him when he dies"; it was not until a few years later, at home in California, that he pounded out the actual *Wild West Weekly* novelette.

Between 1939 and 1954 Tompkins published 27 novels under his own name and one as by Charles Turlock, plus a collection of humorous yarns written for *Zane Grey's Western Magazine* about a character named Justin Other Smith, known as "The Paintin' Pistoleer" because he paints calendars and catalogue covers and is the champeen pistol shot of Arizona Territory. All of these, and all of his pulp stories, were written to a "one-sentence recipe" of his own devising: "Have a worthwhile hero be confronted by an important problem and solve it by his own efforts despite seemingly insurmountable opposition from a strong villain."

Two-Gun also penned numerous nonfiction pieces, including several "how-to" articles on writing Western pulp fiction for *Writer's Digest* in the '30s and '40s; radio dramatizations and motion-picture scenarios; and scripts for "such cultural shows," as he put it, on that old debbil television as *The Cisco Kid*, *The Lone Ranger*, *Cheyenne*, and *Death Valley Days*. In the late '50s he abandoned Western fiction entirely and turned to the fields of regional history (the Santa Barbara, California, area was his specialty), biography, and corporate history. In addition, he maintained a regular newspaper column for the Santa Barbara *News-Press*, a local radio show on historical topics, and a contributing editorship with *Santa Barbara Magazine* until just prior to his death in 1990.

With the exception of "The Paintin' Pistoleer" stories, and a couple of his '50s novels published by Macrae-Smith, all of Tompkins' Westerns were of the hard-core bang-bang variety. "I wasn't ashamed of my stuff being bang-bang," he claimed in 1945, "because I was writing for a juvenile audience—the 10–17 year segment of our population." Even so, by his own admission in 1979, most of his output "was, let's face it, pure crap. Rarely did I ever retype a page of manuscript—it went to the editor exactly as it came out of my head, so of course it lacked polish."

Polish isn't all it lacked. His pulp serials and novelettes and every one of his 11 novels published by Phoenix Press between 1939 and 1944 also lack believable characters, realistic settings, accurate historical contexts, and plots that make much sense. What each does have is a feast of alternative delights. Rarely can one read more than 10 pages of a Two-Gun opus without encountering a character, plot-twist, or passage of prose that induces some degree of hilarity.

Take DESPERADO, for example. First published in England in 1940 under Tompkins' own name and the title SEÑOR DESPERADO: A NOVEL OF OLD CALIFORNIA, it was brought out a year later by Phoenix as by Charles Turlock (for reasons which escape me) and with the shortened one-word title. It is a bang-bang Zorro knock-off—"a rip-roaring tale of the days when California had just been admitted to the Union," according to its jacket blurb, and "men mad for land scoured the country with death and terror." Its protagonist is Frederico Castalina, a grandee who is forced to turn owlhooter by "the cruel lash of the land-grabbers' cunning" and who swears "to wreak vengeance on all thieving gringos." To do this alone would be an impossible job, even for one of Tompkins' heroes, so he forms the Legion of Vengeance, a group composed of men whose ancestral homesteads are being taken from them by treachery and force.

The head "thieving gringo" with whom Castalina is locked in combat throughout is an evil, red-whiskered killer named Curd Rockler. Rockler says things like "Git yore arms up, Castalina! Make a booger move toward them smoke poles, an' thar'll be a dead greaser spillin' his blood hyar—church or no church!" And: "I've met this greaser before, boys. He's the Castalina polecat I told yuh about. An' I'm goin' to shoot him down the same as I would a hydrophoby dog. I'm blastin' you to hell, Señor Desperado!" Rockler usually makes these red-hot pronouncements when "his whiskey-inflamed brain suddenly [goes] berserk with insane wrath," after which he plummets his left hand to a thonged-down holster and brings "a Colt six-gun up, cocked for murder."

The action, of course, is nonstop and hell-roarin'. And it invariably comes complete with italicized sound effects, a Tompkins' (and other bang-bang writers') trademark:

> *Crash!* Frederico's right-hand gun roared deafeningly, and one of the black-whiskered Americanos by the campfire staggered under the impact of a heavy laden ball embedded in his chest.

> *Thud!* Rockler's six-gun slithered from leather and came down across Garcia's skull with a sodden sound. The old Mexican slumped to the floor, eyes glazed with insensibility.

> *Brrang!* A lance of flame spat from the muzzle of Señor Desperado's Colt. And the bullet drilled true and clean through the middle of Curd Rockler's cinnamon-hued mustache.

DESPERADO has other elements to recommend it. Two are inventive sentence structure:

> Camping in a deep barranca, daylight burst over the mountains to find the Legionnaires in saddle.

And a faithful and smart, if timid, watch-horse:

> Then it was that Aguila, the flaxen-tailed palomino, trumpeted a warning as the horse caught sight of Two-Finger Fenton.
> Startled by the note of terror in his mount's whicker, Castalina whirled in time to see Fenton nestling the walnut stock of a doublebarreled weapon to his cheek.

Next we have TROUBLE ON FUNERAL RANGE (1944), a "trigger-fast tale of a gun ace's suspense-packed trail to showdown." The gun ace is young Bob MacQueen, whose first assignment as special guard for the Funeral Range stagecoach and its valuable shipment of gold ends badly when the Comanche Killer and his gang, "the terror of the badlands," ambush the coach in a hail of "drygulchers' bullets [that] scorches the wind." Bob's brother, Sheriff Bruce MacQueen, is croaked in the holdup, but not before he manages to deputize young Bob. And afterward Bob tracks down the outlaw horde with such vengeance that he soon earns the respectful nickname of Deputy Death.

The Comanche Killer is no ordinary bandit, no indeed. For one thing, he wears a mask to hide his identity: "a hideous Indian war-god's mask—a wooden nightmare of reds and blacks and whites—fastened beneath a sinister war bonnet." He dresses in fringed buckskin pants and beaded moccasins, and about his waist is a single gun belt of American make. What the belt holds is a literal pièce de résistance:

> One side of the belt sagged from the weight of the most unusual six-gun Bob MacQueen had ever seen. At first glance, it appeared to be an Indian tomahawk, with red handle and a large flint hatch-ethead.
>
> But MacQueen...knew the terrible history of that tomahawk. In reality, the long handle was a gun barrel, with a rifled bore running its entire length!
>
> The blade of the tomahawk, while its stone edge was used as a hatchet for slaying and wood cutting, was knobbed to fit the big Indian's hand, and served as a pistol stock. Almost hidden by a tuft of hawk feathers where handle met blade was the revolving cylinder of this amazing weapon, which held six cartridges as in any other Colt .45.

If there is a nastier, more inventive, more patently ridiculous hunk of weaponry in all of Western fiction, I've yet to come across it.

The usual gun duels, fistfights, and hair-breadth escapes dominate the story line, including one masterly escape from a candlelit cellar in which Deputy Death has been tied up by the Comanche Killer and which happens to be full of hungry rats "grown to nearly the proportions of gophers." How can he possibly get out of such an impossible situation? Why, by rolling over "until his rope-bound hands were directly beneath the dripping wax of the candle," managing to maneuver so that the falling blobs of tallow land squarely on his knotted ropes, and—

> Five agonizingly slow minutes dragged by, before MacQueen felt the first timid scratch of needle-sharp fangs upon the tallow-soaked ropes of his bonds. Other fangs and claws joined the first rat. Soon fibers began to break, as the rats devoured the rich oil

dropping from the candle upon his ropes. [And finally] he felt a rat-chewed knot give, as biting fangs raveled the hemp.

As alternatively delectable as DESPERADO and TROUBLE ON FUNERAL RANGE are, two other of Two-Gun's Phoenix Press powder-smokers are even wackier. One, THE BORDER EAGLE, we'll examine later. The other is BORDER BONANZA, a 1943 gem that has to be savored in its entirety to be fully appreciated. There is little hint of its wonders in the dust-jacket blurb:

> From Texas to Nevada, Rio Rand and his white mustang Silver Gleam were known to rodeo fans, while the sinister Border Buzzard was equally famous to followers of the owl-hoot trail. When they met, sparks were bound to fly.
>
> Overpowered by the Buzzard's gang and left to die, Rand was rescued by the old prospector Cactus Kinlay, and learned the secret of the fabulously wealthy, long-lost Crescent Moon Mine. Unluckily, the Buzzard too overheard. And the long and desperate struggle for the bonanza which ensued involved the bloodiest, grimmest gun play which had ever sent its echoes ricocheting up from the streets of Bullet Gap.

The secret of the Crescent Moon Mine has to do with some pieces of dagger blade "engraved with mystic Spanish writing. When the entire blade was pieced together, it would form the key to the location of the...long-lost treasure place of the ancient Spanish padres who had explored Arizona's badlands hundreds of years before." (Sound a bit similar to the long-lost treasure in Archie Joscelyn's GUNS OF LOST VALLEY? No surprise there. Fabulous lost treasures of ancient padres and conquistadors crop up in dozens of bang-bang novels and pulp stories, usually hidden in caves, caverns, or subterranean grottos.)

In addition to the Border Buzzard, whose real name is Garl Lemardo, there are hardcases galore in the pages of this epic, all of whom have names like Injun Joe, Ferg Slake, and Snag Roke. There are locales called Snaketrail Gorge, the Plugged Peso Saloon, and the House o' Death Saloon. There is a raucous Saturday-night dance known as the Boot Hill Ball. There are dynamite bombs, a narrow escape from a bed of quicksand, some gold loot cannily hidden by outlaws inside an ant hill, a knife fight, and numerous shootouts accompanied by Batman-style sound effects: *Crash!*, *Bam!*, *Brrong!*, *Smack!*, *Slam!*, *Spang!*, and *Boom!*, among others. There is a climactic scene in which Rio Rand, "who did not hold the rodeo-shooting championship of the West for nothing," blasts a crimson hole in the middle of the Border Buzzard's brain pan. And of course there is an abundance of such dialogue as:

> "Me go now," grunted the Yaqui, seeing that his mescal bottle was drained dry. "Me go whet up knife."
>
> Garl Lemardo shot out a restraining hand to grasp Injun Joe's leather-hued wrist.
>
> "You don't even know yet what you're supposed to do when you kill him!" snarled the outlaw in Spanish. "Rand has something on him that I want, savvy?"
>
> "Me savvy," grunted Injun Joe. "Me ketch um Rio Rand at fiesta tonight. Git him in dark place, stick um knife heap deep. Me git pieces of dagger blade for you, yeah."

But BORDER BONANZA's truly distinguishing feature, the one that makes it a tour-de-force among alternative Western classics, is Tompkins' portrayal of his hero, "Ridin' Rand of the Rio Grande," and Rand's horse Silver Streak (not Silver Gleam, in spite of the jacket blurb). Each is described thusly in the early pages, after they are ambushed by the Border Buzzard and his sidewindin' pards:

> The horse's white coat gleamed like polished silver in the sunlight, which also glinted off the silver trappings of a red saddle, tapaderos, bridle and ornamented martingale....

> [Rand's] sombrero was a white Stetson with a band of glittering Indian beadwork, as red as rubies. About his throat was looped a bright red bandanna, which matched the star-shaped red pockets and red cuffs of his white rodeo shirt.
>
> Rand's lean, powerful legs were incased in white buckskin trousers and expensive boots of kangaroo leather, white even to the spike heels and inlaid with a red leather design of the face and spreading horns of a Texas steer.
>
> Girding his waist were two white gun belts, studded with .45 cartridges and supporting white leather holsters. The stocks of

Rand's two .45s bore out his unique color scheme—they were of the vivid red material used to make pool balls.

Crrash! Brrong! Western fiction's first rhinestone cowboy!

No wonder Rio worries that the Border Buzzard's crowd will "be gangin' me before many more minutes." No wonder people keep trying to kill him everywhere he goes: He never once changes his costume, not in town nor on the trail nor riding roughshod through barrancas and along mountain cliffs.

In the real Arizona border country of the 1880s, a gent who blithely went around on a gaudy silver-ornamented horse, wearing a cute red-and-white outfit and spike-heeled kangaroo-leather boots with a Texas-steer design, would have lasted about two minutes. Give or take a few ticks. And there wouldn't have been enough left of him to bother with a Boot Hill burial, much less to put on display at the Boot Hill Ball.

And then out of the blue it came. The incredible, the blasting menace that brought death in a flight of arrows: hideous din as the blood-chilling howl of the redmen mounted tragedy on the brooding summer moon—over the ridge poured mounted redskins like echoing demons of the deadly-twanging arrows, and the stage horses raced their human charges into panic reaction as the guard, with a pierced throat, hit the rump of one of the wheelers in his plunge to the earth, and his rifle roared once, impotently, as it hit the trail. —Saul Anthony, "Gunsmoke Medicine"

3. "Hoppin' Horned Jibblenippers!"

For much of the first half of this century, pulp magazines were the leading supplier of popular fiction—not only in the U.S. but in Canada and England as well. Successors to the dime novels and story weeklies of the 19th century, they provided inexpensive escapist reading for imaginative young adults and the so-called "common man," selling for a nickel or a dime in their early years and a quarter in their final ones. At the height of their popularity, in the mid-'30s, there were more than 200 different titles on the newsstands.

Far and away the most popular pulps were Westerns. Such titles as *Western Story, Wild West Weekly, Ranch Romances, Texas Rangers,* and *Dime Western* perennially outsold those in all other categories throughout most of the pulp era. The first Western pulp was established by Street & Smith, the dime-novel kings. In 1919 S&S revamped one of their dime-novel periodicals, *New Buffalo Bill Weekly,* into the 7-by-10-inch pulp format and retitled the new biweekly *Western Story Magazine.* (At that time pulp magazines had been around for nearly 20 years. Frank A. Munsey had restructured *Argosy* into a pulp in the mid-1890s, and soon afterward brought out numerous other pulp titles, among them *All-Story Weekly, Popular Magazine,* and *The Railroad Man's Magazine.*) The circulation of *Western Story,* which sold for 10 cents, burgeoned in the '20s, when Street & Smith made it into a weekly, and it remained one of the two or three top-selling titles over most of its three decades of life.

Western Story's success inspired the usual run of imitations and variations. Doubleday brought out *West* and *Frontier Stories*, which would also prove to be long-running titles; William Clayton started *Cowboy Stories, Ace-High Western, Ranch Romances*, and *Western Adventures;* Fiction House produced *Lariat;* and S&S added *Far West*, among others, to its string. In the '30s Ned Pines and his editorial director, Leo Margulies, started Standard Magazines and its Thrilling group, which included *Thrilling Western, Popular Western, Texas Rangers, The Rio Kid Western, Masked Rider Western*, and *Range Riders Western*. Harry Steeger's Popular Publications, eventually the largest and most active of the pulp-chain outfits, also jumped on the bandwagon with *Dime Western, .44 Western, New Western, Star Western*, and *Big-Book Western*. And there were numerous other titles produced by independent and small-chain companies, a few of which flourished for a while but most of which were short-lived; among these were *Ace Western* and *Mammoth Western.*

Some Western pulps—notably, S&S's *Western Story*—were aimed at a reasonably literate adult audience. Others, however, were packaged and written for a young and less demanding readership. The unabashed justification for this was summed up by Walker Tompkins in 1945: "Every year in America a generation of 10-year-old kids start devouring Western fiction. They want to supplement their reading of the comic magazines with cowboy stories. And they want blood to flow and six-guns to bark on every page."

Nearly all of Standard Magazines' Western titles fell into this rarefied category, as did Clayton's *Cowboy Stories* and *Ace-High*, Popular's *Star Western*, and Street & Smith's *Wild West Weekly* and *Wild West Stories & Complete Novel Magazine*. Their main fare was the cow-country yarn, in which "brave, chivalrous, admirable heroes fight desperate, unscrupulous villains," as Leo Margulies says in his 1935 introduction to WESTERN THRILLERS. He goes on to describe these stories as having "plenty of gun-fighting, ranch and range activities, with physical action motivating a swift-moving yarn to a logical conclusion." A pulp editor's definition of "logical conclusion," of course, usually meant nothing more than bloody but unbowed hero triumphant and unscrupulous villain dead in the dust.

Western heroes, particularly series heroes, were invariably "laconic, lean, strong on decency and ethical codes," in the words of pulp authority Robert Sampson; they were also fast on the shoot, hell on wheels in a fistfight, noble and shy around women, kind to horses and dogs, and quick to champion lost causes and the plight of the downtrodden. Many were lawdogs of one stripe or another: sheriffs, U.S. marshals, Texas and Arizona rangers, Cattlemen's Association detectives, railroad dicks. Of these, several had their own magazines in which their wild and woolly adventures were chronicled monthly by various authors writing under a single house name. The first was Pete Rice, the sheriff of Buzzard Gap, Arizona, who with the aid of a pair of part-time deputies, Misery Hicks and Teeny Butler (Western pulp heroes always had at least one sidekick, usually outspoken types with quaint monikers whose main purpose was to provide backup firepower and comic relief), battled his way through dozens of perilous odysseys in *Pete Rice Magazine* from 1933 to 1935 and in *Wild West Weekly* until 1939.

The most popular of the superhero lawmen was Jim Hatfield, "the long-legged Ranger galoot" who was also known as the Lone Wolf; he appeared in some 200 novellas in *Texas Rangers* over a nearly 20-year span. These were published under the house name Jackson Cole and mainly written, after 1937, by A. Leslie Scott, the father of contemporary best-selling suspense writer Justin Scott. Numerous other industrious scribblers also contributed Hatfield tales, among them Oscar Schisgall, Tom Curry, Walker Tompkins, and Charles N. Heckleman.

Additional superlawdogs of note were range detective Steve Reese and his pards Hank Ball and Dusty Trail (who had a "keen, hair-trigger brain" and whose favorite expression was "Bellerin' bullfrogs!"), the featured players of *Range Riders Western;* The Lone Ranger (yes, he of "Hi-yo Silver" and the faithful Tonto), who had his own magazine for a brief eight issues in 1937; and The Pecos Kid, star of another short-run publication (five issues in 1950–51), *The Pecos Kid Western,* and the creation of Dan Cushman.

There were outlaw heroes, too (all unjustly accused and branded, naturally), such as Ward M. Stevens' Sonny Tabor, who was "plumb full of vinegar and hell smoke" and who made frequent appearances in the pages of *Wild West Weekly* in the '20s and '30s; cowboy heroes, such as George C. Henderson's Whizz Fargo, a "hard-ridin', straight shootin' waddy" whose partner's name was Hopdoodle O'Day; wandering do-gooders such as The Rio Kid, created by Tom Curry, who in his peripatetic adventures becomes involved with real historical figures such as Custer, Wild Bill Hickok, Calamity Jane, Wyatt Earp, and Judge Roy Bean; and masked Zorro-type heroes, such as Guy Maynard's Señor Red Mask.

There were even a couple of Indian knights: Vincente, the Yaqui, "a magnificent hunk of Indian manhood" who rode a horse named Tortilla; and White Eagle, a blond Comanche warrior who starred in Red Star's *Big Chief Western*—a fearsome figure who could "shave the whiskers of a frog at twenty paces with an ax and not even frighten the frog" and with a war arrow "cut off the frog's tail without drawing blood."

And finally, there was (gasp!) a female hero: Señorita Scorpion, "a hell for leather woman" ranch owner and masked avenger whose escapades in *Frontier Stories* are several notches above the average Western-hero fare, owing to the fact that most were written by Les Savage, Jr., one of the best of the Western pulpsters.

The redoubtable *Wild West Weekly* featured more series cavaliers than any other magazine during its two decades of existence. Sonny Tabor and Pete Rice were the readers' top hands. Whizz Fargo, Freckles Malone, The Silver Kid, The Oklahoma Kid, Jim Tate (whose partner, Windy, was forever yapping "Hoppin' horned jibblenippers!"), Flash Moran, Jim-Twin Allen (a.k.a. The White Wolf), Rowdy Lang, Silver Jack Steel, Risky McKee, Blacky Solone, Rawride Runyan, and Walker Tompkins' Border Eagle are just a few of the others who enjoyed varying degrees of favor.

My alternative favorite, though, is Andrew A. Griffin's Johnny Forty-five. Dozens of yarns featuring this pint-sized U.S. Deputy Marshal and his sidekick, fat and boastful George Krumm (a.k.a. Iron Man Krumm, a.k.a. Fearless Krumm, the Terror of Evildoers), appeared in the magazine in the '30s and '40s. John Socrates Forty-five, which we are told is his real name, has a brash manner, a jaunty swagger, and a lightning-fast draw of the heavy-caliber Colts he keeps tucked into well-oiled, thong-tied holsters. But he would be just another run-of-the-mill star-toter if it weren't for a special character quirk (some might justifiably say character flaw). Most of the pulp superstuds had quirks of one ilk or another, to separate them from their brethren, but none is in a class with Johnny Forty-five's. Johnny, you see, fancies himself—as obviously did his creator—to be a poet.

At least a dozen times per story, at opportune and inopportune moments alike, while dealing with good folks and evildoers, he bursts forth with four-line rhymes of allegedly witty and pithy nature. It was Andrew Griffin's contention that these bits of dog-gerel, in addition to being Johnny Forty-five's trademark, were composed on the spur of the moment, with the same lightning-like speed as our hero's gundraw. George Krumm doesn't much care for his pard's whimsical flights of poesy; neither do most other characters whom the pair encounters. In fact, given the content of some of the rhymes, it is surprising that the long-suffering Fearless Krumm, with or without assistance, failed to string old Johnny up by his tongue.

Here is John Socrates "lifting his voice in a lilting carol" in a 1936 story called "Johnny Forty-five's Iron Trail":

> "I listened to yore story,
> And I think yuh'd better hush,
> Yuh may not be a liar,
> But yuh'd make a liar blush."

And here he is spouting off even more alternatively in a pair of 1942 novelettes, first in "Where Sheriffs Fear to Tread":

> "Hurry with that breakfast, George;
> Let's hear that java pur [sic]!

I'm hungry enough to eat my boot,
And pick my teeth with the spur!"

"Grin while the grinnin' is good, Bart,
For before this deal is over,
You'll lose a trick in graveyard spades,
And snooze beneath the clover."

"All this about the Scorpion, sir,
Won't make me fret or groan.
A Scorp is a bug with a stinger,
But I've a couple here of my own."

"Dead or alive is my orders,
Take your choices, you smelly foxes!
You'll either go a-standin' up,
Or you'll go in coffin boxes."

And then in "Ruin to Renegades!":

"If you want to improve your shootin'
Here's the way, I quoth:
Instead of closin' one eye
Why don't you shut 'em both?"

"It's just a little thing I do
To exercise the trigger finger;
If I should get the roomatiz,
My soul on earth not long would linger."

"Up with your dirty gunhooks!
You're through with murders and wrecks!
There's some empty nooses waitin',
And they'll soon be full of necks!"

"Take it, you murderin' skunkaroo!
It's a slug, and I'm hopin' it suits;
It's got your name wrote on it,
So die in your smelly boots!"

🐎 🐎 🐎 🐎

Just as interesting to the alternative mind are the Western-pulp villains. These fall into two categories: superbaddies and your average, two-brain-cell gun-thug. Supervillains are invariably smart, more than a little cracked, suffer from megalomania and a slavering hunger for power and control. They organize and lead large gangs and are constantly devising schemes to steal vast sums of money, find and steal lost treasures, and/or take over ranches, valleys, towns, or entire territories. Many are natural-born geologists, in that they are somehow able to find one of those old standbys, a cave or cavern or subterranean grotto in which to hide out from all except the superheroes who spell their doom. Quite a few lead double lives, masquerading as honest citizens, and thus wear masks—usually of an elaborate variety such as Walker Tompkins' Comanche Killer's Injun mask—to conceal their identities while they go about their nefarious business. They also seem to have had repressed childhoods in which their parents refused them the privilege of setting off Fourth of July fireworks, since one of their favorite pastimes is blowing up people and things with dynamite.

No pulp fictioneer created more unusual and improbable supervillains than Two-Gun Tompkins. In scores of yarns he hurled lunatic after lunatic at his presumably adoring readers, especially those who followed the monthly adventures of Standard Magazines' stable of superheroes. In at least half of the lead novels he wrote for *Masked Rider Western, Range Riders Western,* and *Texas Rangers,* a masked and/or power-mad whacko is the chief adversary.

A random example is Chief Red Eagle, outlaw leader of "The Renegades of Robber's Roost" (*Range Riders Western,* March 1947). "A figure of sinister mystery throughout Montana," Red Eagle is believed to be a Sioux Indian, a fugitive from a reservation in the eastern part of the Territory where General Custer had been wiped out a generation before. In addition to robbing and plundering, his main goal in life is to wipe out all the ranchers in Riverford Valley because they want to build a dam on Glacier River, whose waters would back up and eventually flood Red Eagle's lair in a cave in a high mountain valley in the Thundergust Range.

> The leader of Robber's Roost looked like something out of a nightmare. A hefty man, he wore buckskin leggings and elkhide moccasins. His barrel chest was covered with a brushpopper's jacket and criss-crossed with cartridge bandoliers.
>
> But his mask, the grotesque creation of an Ogallala Sioux witchdoctor, was what put Red Eagle into a class with an ogre straight out of the underworld. It was a typical medicine man's mask, made of shaggy buffalo hide fitted with slots for eye-holes. Twin cow horns jutted from the top of the mask, making Red Eagle resemble a devil.

A pretty formidable foe for Steve Reese and his pards, you will admit. Particularly since Chief Red Eagle is even more enamored of explosives than most supernuts; he would rather blow things up —with wagonloads of dynamite, not just a few sticks—than rob, plunder, or strut around Robber's Roost scaring the bejesus out of the case-hardened outlaws who pay him their allegiance. Unfortunately, Tompkins spoils the sinister effect somewhat by allowing the chief to have a voice and to use it often. Two-Gun was a whiz at creating villains and screwball situations, but when it came to writing ethnic dialogue he had an ear so tinny it must have rusted in a rainstorm. How can you take seriously an Injun miscreant, even one who looks like an ogre straight out of the underworld, when he says things like—

> "This wagon box is caulked like um boat. We set um wagon afloat in river. It floats down canyon, comes to stop against the dam which threatens to drown us like rats. A thirty-thirty bullet in this box of percussion caps explode um heap quick. Caps blow up, touch off dynamite. *Whoof!* Blast blow um dam to blazes, let water empty out of canyon."

> "This man heap bad! He no killer from Texas. This man live-um big lie. His real name is Dusty Trail, and he is heap bad detective for Cattleman's Protective Association, come to spy on camp of Red Eagle! Ugh!"

Ugh, indeed.

Your average gun-thug is also easy to identify in a bang-bang pulp story. Unlike the superwicked types, he isn't provided with a colorful sobriquet like Chief Red Eagle or Señor Diablo or the Border Buzzard. Nor, for that matter, is he christened with one of the quaint handles bestowed upon heroic sidekicks, bowlegged cowhands, and grizzled prospectors—names such as Doleful Dave Tunkett, Hi Grab Haines, Snaggle-Tooth Potter, Soapy Waters, Muttonballs Griswold, Snoozin' Ed Vrigo, Bat-Wing Bowles, Dork Wallace, and Old Whang Witherall. But what the average gun-thug *is* forced to wear like a badge of dishonor is a harsh, nasty name that immediately stamps him as a deadly, noose-dodging leadslinger. Snake Belcher, for instance. Or Slag Worgo. Or Lynx Merson. Or Slats Terminal. Or Grizzly Greetch. Or Fink Borsht. Or Scar-mouth Leach. Or The Wart.

But none of these can hold a smoking hogleg to the evil jasper who appears in a 1936 *Wild West Weekly* story by Whizz Fargo's papa, George C. Henderson, called "Quick-Trigger Luck." This shaggy-haired, drunken cutthroat whose guns are for hire to the highest bidder, who is as thin as a snake and has spindly legs and a small head and "bony features mottled and red with killer rage and drink," who drools between lips drawn back from sharp, pointed rodent teeth, who growls such red-hot palaver as "Smoke 'em up, yuh long-legged star toter!" just before he starts smokin' 'em up himself, is by far the orneriest, meanest hyderphobia skunk ever to draw brief breath in the crumbling pages of a Western-pulp magazine. And he has a name to match, by God, the meanest, nastiest, most spectacular handle in all of bang-bang outlawry.

Viper Snarl.

Viper Snarl!

Take a few seconds to roll that name around and under your tongue, before you spit it out like a mouthful of bad tonsil polish. Then take another few seconds to imagine what must surely have been some vermin-infested desert hovel inhabited by the Snarl family, and a post-partum conversation between the begatters of the ugliest, nastiest baby ever born of man and woman.

Mrs. Snarl: "What'll we call this miserable dang bundle of slobber?"

Mr. Snarl (laughing evilly): "Let's really mess with the little booger's head. Let's call him Viper. Then we'll sit back and watch the fun."

Psycho mom, psycho dad. I mean, how could somebody named Viper Snarl *not* grow up to be an ornery, drunken, drooling cutthroat packed to the brim with killer rage?

🐎 🐎 🐎 🐎

The paper shortage of World War II killed off a large number of pulp titles, including a score of marginal Western books. Of the survivors, a handful were purchased by the healthier chain outfits such as Popular and Standard and thus underwent changes in editorial policy. A few new titles were introduced during and after the war, and into the early '50s, among them two named after Western-pulp giants: *Max Brand's Western Magazine* and *Walt Coburn's Western Magazine,* both Popular titles.

But the handwriting was on the wall: The pulps were doomed. The advent of war may have ended the Great Depression, but it also began the decline and fall of the pulp kingdom; and in the war's aftermath, things began to change rapidly and radically everywhere. The publishing industry was especially vulnerable. Television and paperback books were the coming forms of inexpensive entertainment; there was little room for the pulps (or for their cousins, the lending-library publishers) in the new and changing society.

Most titles were extinct by 1952. A few hardy ones, mostly Westerns, hung on a few years longer: *Dime Western, Thrilling Western, Big-Book Western, Fifteen Western Tales,* and *.44 Western* until 1954; *Western Short Stories, Complete Western Book, Texas Rangers,* and *2-Gun Western* until 1957–58. *Ranch Romances,* amazingly enough, lasted until 1970 (though it was a mere shadow of itself at the end, publishing reprints almost exclusively), thus earning the distinction of being the longest-surviving pulp title.

Although technically not pulp magazines, the digest-size Western periodicals of the past 50 years were in fact pulps in every major respect: aim, content, even the paper on which they were printed. The only appreciable difference was size. The first title to appear in this format was the short-lived *Pocket Western* of the late '30s, but it was Street & Smith that had the first success with the digest size. During World War II S&S decided to conserve paper by shrinking such long-standing pulp titles as *Western Story* and *Romantic Range* (and *Detective Story, Doc Savage*, and *The Shadow*). The pocket format proved so popular with readers that even after the war S&S continued to publish *Western Story* as a digest, until its demise in 1949.

Other publishers followed Street & Smith's lead in reducing full-size magazines to the smaller form. One was Robert A.W. Lowndes' Columbia Publications, which in 1957 shrank *Famous Western* and in 1958 reduced *Double-Action Western, Western Action*, and *Real Western;* these remained digest size until Columbia's group demise in 1960. From an alternative perspective, Lowndes' books are the most interesting of the Western digests. They were the *Wild West Weekly* and *Cowboy Stories* of their era, offering formula Western tales of the lowest order.

By the late '50s most of the prolific bang-bang contributors had died off, retired, or elevated their output to meet contemporary tastes; a few recognizable pulp names contributed a story or two to Columbia's line—Noel Loomis, William Hopson, Roe Richmond —and Lee Floren was a frequent contributor under a variety of names, but Columbia paid too poorly to entice regular submissions from most of the remaining old-timers. Lowndes, therefore, had to rely primarily on work produced by unknowns, bottom-of-the-barrel hacks, and young "crossover" writers whose main output was in the fields of mystery and science fiction but who could be persuaded to try their hands at a Western. (The last group included Harlan Ellison, Edward D. Hoch, and Robert Silverberg.)

For the most part, the contents pages of *Famous Western, Western Action*, and other Columbia horse-opera publications were jammed with names unfamiliar elsewhere, before or since: William F. Schwartz, Olin Grant, Harlan Clay, H. C. Early, Earle Sayles Bennett, Wallace McKinley, Ruel McDaniel, Cos Barat, Saul Anthony, Art Cleveland, D. L. Hyde, Bradley Burr, Rueben Jenner, Cleve Curran, Julius Elman, Roscoe A. Poland, Sigmund H. Kalina, Ell Emm Moore, and Hanan Zeus.

Those among this glittering array who were actual people (some of the names are surely pseudonyms) produced works of alternative merit, but only one stands out: Saul Anthony. Whoever he was, his talent was awesome. "Outlaws of Dust Canyon" (*Double-Action Western,* August 1959) is wonderfully bad, but a "short novel" called "Gunsmoke Medicine," which appeared in *Western Action* for May 1959, is a howling blue-whistler.

For one thing, it makes so little sense that one wonders if anyone at Columbia bothered to read it. If it *was* read by Lowndes or an assistant, then the only possible excuse for buying and publishing it is that they were desperate for stories to fill that month's issue. "Gunsmoke Medicine"'s accompanying editorial blurb asks, "Why were Indians in peaceful territory suddenly attacking the stage coach?"—a perfectly rational question for which Anthony fails to provide a rational answer.

Set in New Mexico, the story seems to have something to do with a plan by a Texas "gun-waddy" named Blackie Brill to break a long-standing Navajo treaty by dressing himself and his band of outlaws up in Apache garb ("Don't ask me what Apaches are doing in Navajo country," Anthony brilliantly has one of his characters say early on in the narrative) in order to make the local whites think the redskins are on the warpath so he, Blackie Brill, can steal their land so he can get his dew-claws on some gold hidden in a cave under "a great freak of nature" called the Devil's Courtroom.

Pitted against this villainous gent is the sheriff of Paradise Hole, "Gunsmoke" Gunn, who rides "a huge Roman-nosed sorrel," and Louise Sinfer, a "young miss from back east" who loses her beautiful red hair, not to mention her bonnet and the rest of her clothing during an "Injun" attack in the opening pages, said hair and said clothing then being put on a murdered cavalry escort who gets booted out of the stage into a rock-strewn chasm just before the coach crashes and Louise, who is also known as "Miss Five Feet Nothing," is saved by a cavalry officer named McHenry, or possibly by Gunsmoke Gunn dressed up in Navajo garb himself, take your pick.

Clear so far? There is lots of shooting and lots of running around, and plenty of description of Paradise Hole and the Devil's Courtroom and the cave and various characters, but none of this makes much sense, either, because Saul Anthony wrote English as if it were his second or third language and he was thus forced to consult either a dictionary or a thesaurus or both every other sentence, and even then he didn't really understand what he was reading, much less what he was putting down on paper, and also failed to grasp the proper usage of punctuation, especially the period, which lack of understanding resulted in incredible strings of run-on sentences not quite as long as this one but almost.

This chapter's epigraph is one example of Anthony's prose. Here are some others, beginning with "Gunsmoke Medicines"'s opening sentence.

> The stage from Santa Fe kept its monotonous position at the head of the fast-traveling ribbon of dust that settled in its wake, and the brilliant-hued landscape continued to swallow the drumming of its clattering passing with the brooding indifference of the ancient land that the whites had called New Mexico.

> No one man would pull the horses up this side of the river now, but as he burst feet-first through the off-side door of the stage his actions were part of a sequence that brooked neither thought nor alternative, for there was time for nothing except that one dominating strategy that would fail or flourish in the mad seconds as the stage denied the galloping warriors its immediate capture in its rocketing bolt.

> Without warning, the big figure who had slipped from the uneasy coach to the immovable solidity of the big granite boulder, stepped to its top as the clattering and ugly cavalcade commenced to open out round the coach, and deafening echoes of Colt fire blat-blat-blatted in a sonorous roll that enveloped the river scene; emptied saddles; created havoc, and panicked Apache survivors into precipitate retreat.

> The big figure on the boulder took almost deliberate choice, launched himself on to a big pinto in the same movement as he

hammered a Colt butt against its Apache ex-owner's skull, and next moment appeared in a cloud of spray at the swinging door of the stage.

Big Byrne Elk's rather laborious effort to try and out-think whatever opposition the gang was up against was assisted, he thought, by the sight of the new stage-line depot manager eating his evening meal at Malone's Eats, in company with a couple of his regular customers, right in the most prominent spot just inside the hash-house's entrance. Elk waved a greeting at the manager as he rode past and the manager didn't contradict him in any way partly because his mouth was full of hash and partly because a Colt barrel beneath the table was prodding him in the spot the hash was bound for and it seemed a shame to waste it.

🐎 🐎 🐎 🐎

In addition to the shrunken pulp titles, numerous Western magazines were born as digests. Two carried Zane Grey's name in their titles. The first, *Zane Grey's Western Magazine*, was arguably the best of all the Western-fiction monthlies. Under the editorship of Don Ward, it debuted in November of 1946 and over the next eight years published original stories by most of the major names in the field, notable reprints, and first stories by such luminaries as Elmore Leonard.

The second version, *Zane Grey Western Magazine* (without the possessive), was established in 1969 by Leo Margulies as part of his Renown Publications string (which also included *Mike Shayne Mystery Magazine*, *Shell Scott Mystery Magazine*, and *The Man from U.N.C.L.E.*). Margulies' *ZGWM* had a life of just under four years, only the first two of which were as a digest; in its final years it was issued bimonthly and transformed into the large, flat format of such magazines as *True West*, and devoted as much space to fact articles as to fiction.

The Margulies incarnation featured a novella in each issue based on such Zane Grey characters as Arizona Ames, Buck Duane, and Laramie Nelson, which were purportedly written by Grey's son, Romer. In fact, they were penned by veteran Western fictioneers such as Tom Curry, and by overeager and callow newcomers. Easily the worst of these pulp-styled novellas is a thing called "The Raid at Three Rapids," which appeared in the November 1970 issue.

Billed as "A Novel of Wild Western Trails," it features Arizona Ames—or rather a bang-bang version of Grey's cowhand, drifter, and gunfighter that likely would have sent his creator into a snarling snit if he'd known about it. In this *ZGWM* deviation, Ames accepts an assignment to work as a special undercover agent for Arizona Territorial Governor James Cardwell. Accepts the assignment without question, for "he didn't have to know the reason; it was sufficient that he had been asked. His nickname, after all, was Arizona."

Eventually, though, he learns the reason: A dam is being built on the mythical Sangre River, in mythical Gila Basin near the mythical town of Three Rapids, an erection so vital that when completed it will turn the entire basin from arid wasteland into a "fertile belt" for farms and ranches and thus help earn statehood for Arizona. The fly in the ointment is a band of nightriders that is terrorizing the small ranchers in the basin and thus threatening to undermine the vital dam project. It is Ames' job to ferret out the purpose behind the reign of terror, unmask the gang's leader, and thus save the day for all the good folk concerned.

Ah, but the nightriders are no ordinary gang of thieves and murdering sidewinders. No, indeed. They're ghosts. That is, they seem to be ghosts—wraithlike, glow-in-the-dark figures on skeletal glow-in-the-dark horses, who ride out from and then disappear back into a nearby burial ground. The bone orchard is known as Superstition Cemetery because it's supposed to be sacred and left undisturbed, and the alleged reason for the "ghosts" taking it into their bony heads to go out marauding is that the cemetery, their resting place, will be inundated and destroyed once the dam is built.

This is how one of the ectoplasmic killers is described in an early scene:

> There, framed in the doorway, was a hideous, grinning specter. A glowing skeleton, topped by a death's head with fire-brand sockets

for eyes, its fleshless mouth ripped back in a wild, demoniacally fiendish grin.

And from the depths of whatever hell had spawned the ghost rose a hollow, chilling laugh which curdled the marrow.

Pretty scary stuff, right? But not to Arizona Ames; he's equal to the task of proving that the raiders are not supernatural beings but vicious human gun-hombres. The editorial blurb introducing the story states it even more eloquently: "Ghost riders? Arizona Ames grunted. 'Ghost riders don't tote no .45s. I'm riding down after those varmints!'"

And ride down after them he does, through flurries of gun-hail on a train, in the town of Three Rapids, on a ranch in Gila Basin, and in Superstition Cemetery. Before the gunsmoke finally clears, he has exposed the leader of the gang to be a local lunatic banker whose secret passion is to become Governor of the Sovereign State of Arizona and whose mad plan involved halting the construction of the Sangre River Dam for six months, during which time he would foreclose on the mortgages of all the small landowners in the Basin so that when the land becomes fertile and productive after the dam is built, it would be worth a fortune and he'd own the whole shebang. Ames also exposes the ghost gimmick, which of course is nothing more than costume flummery:

> The mask was thickly painted with a heavy luminous dye, more than likely radium based, so as to give it the appearance of a grinning death's head. There were two small slits for eyeholes. [The] clothing was all black as well, a lightweight shirt, trousers, leather gloves, heavy boots, and all of it save for the boots had been similarly painted with bonelike designs that would make [the wearer], from a distance, resemble a ghostly, skeletal apparition. He also wore, rolled high up on his back and across his shoulder, a thick-weaved black ulster. This garment was unadorned.

But the greatest alternative element in this 20,000-word cow flop is the hideout used by the ghost killers and the method by which they were able to vanish inside Superstition Cemetery. It seems that the cemetery contains a huge crypt, built by a rich and crazy miner: "Stark and gray, of neo-Grecian design, with a sloped roof and three huge, ornate Corinthian pillars fronting it. The bleak coldness of the structure seemed to cast a pall of foreboding, of malevolence, over the entire graveyard." Around to the rear of the crypt is a secret entrance, which is opened by pressing down on a miner's pick on a column of bas-relief etchings: "The complete rear wall slowly tilted on some unseen axis and without a hesitant motion, rose as one solid piece." Inside is a bier with another hidden lever on it, and when Ames presses that one down—

> The same silent rumbling sound emitted from the tomb, and then it began to swing back on one corner, not stopping until it rested against the far wall.
>
> It was like opening a cavern to hell. A wide, stone-hewn ramp led downward from where Arizona Ames stood by the bier.... The ramp, wide enough for horses and riders, gently leveled out. A rider, hunched over his mount, could pass through here. Once the passages were lit with firebrands, the way would be clear for the galloping hordes of "ghost" killers to come and go quickly.

And exactly where is it they go? Why, into a huge subterranean grotto, of course. Seems that entire section of Superstition Cemetery "is honeycombed with underground shafts and passageways. The old miner owned the claim to the area, and had the crypt built right on top of all the mine tunneling." Why did the old miner build the crypt with a secret entrance and a secret passageway into the underground shafts? "He was queer for secret passages and the like," one of the ghost killers explains. But the real reason, we later learn, is that the old miner "was always talkin' about bein' buried alive, on account of a mining accident when he was a button.... I guess that can change a man some."

So can reading alternative twaddle like the foregoing.

So can writing alternative twaddle like the foregoing.

It was not, you see, just one overeager and callow newcomer who perpetrated "The Raid at Three Rapids" under the guise of Romer Zane Grey; it was two, working shamelessly in tandem. One was Jeff Wallmann, who has more or less put his lurid past behind him and is now teaching at the University of Nevada in Reno.

The other, alas, was me.

"Thundering mustangs!" exclaimed Wes, pointing judicially with his leathery whip butt at the creamy bronco with the girl of super whiteness atop. "Who's your blinding lady friend, Bob? Talk about sun worshippers! Yon girl must be the center of the solar system!"

—Samuel Alexander White, NORTHWEST PATROL

4. The Bull Moose and Other Scourges of the Frozen North

"Northerns"—tales set in the rough-and-tumble frontier days of Alaska, the Yukon, the Canadian Barrens, the Hudson's Bay region—were a popular adjunct of the Western story during the first half of this century. The widespread publicity given to the Yukon Gold Rush of 1897–98 and the Alaska Gold Rush a few years later focused attention on that part of the world and stirred the imaginations of armchair as well as actual adventurers. Among the thousands who flocked to the Northland were Jack London and Rex Beach, who went in search of story material as well as precious metal; other writers, such as Robert W. Service and James B. Hendryx, also visited Alaska and the Yukon in the years following the stampedes. Such novels as London's CALL OF THE WILD, Beach's THE SPOILERS, and Service's THE TRAIL OF '98—and Service's stirring collection of poems, THE CALL OF THE YUKON—became best-sellers. These in turn spawned thousands of adventure stories and novels and numerous films featuring Far North prospectors, fur trappers, wilderness pilots and explorers, dog-sledders, traders, gamblers, saloonkeepers, outlaws, and officers of the Northwest Mounted Police.

So popular were Northerns in the period between the two World Wars that entire pulp magazines such as *North-West Stories* (later *Northwest Romances*), *Real Northwest Stories,* and *Complete Northwest Novel* were devoted entirely or in large part to what were billed variously as "Big Outdoor Stories of the West and North," "Stories of the Wilderness Frontier," and "Vigorous, Tingling Epics of the Great Snow Frontier." *North-West Stories* acquired such a loyal following that it lasted considerably longer than most pulps, nearly 30 years (1925–1952). Northerns could also be found in many issues of such adventure pulps as *Short Stories*, *Adventure*, *Argosy*, *Blue Book*, and *Action Stories;* in several of the Western titles, notably Street & Smith's *Western Story;* in such slick-paper periodicals as *Collier's*, *Liberty*, and *The Saturday Evening Post;* and even now and then, surprisingly, in such publications as *Coronet*, which seldom used fiction.

Substantial literary careers were built by men specializing in the Northern-adventure yarn. James Oliver Curwood, author of such novels as THE ALASKAN and the story collection BACK TO GOD'S COUNTRY, was the most prominent. Another of note was James B. Hendryx, who published 36 novels and collections with Alaska and Yukon settings; his long-running series featuring Black John Smith, leader of an outlaw community on Halfaday Creek who dispenses his own brand of swift justice to those less scrupulous than he, had a large following in such pulps as *Adventure* and *Short Stories* and in book form (the 13 Black John collections published between 1935 and 1953 are highly prized by modern collectors). Other practitioners include George Marsh, who wrote acclaimed stories of the Hudson's Bay country; Robert Ormond Case, creator of an excellent series of novels about a pilot, remittance man, and adventurer named Ravenhill; and William Byron Mowery, who concocted stories about Mounties, wilderness treks, and Northland mystery with equal aplomb.

Prominent writers of traditional Westerns occasionally took a flyer at a Northern, some with satisfactory results: William MacLeod Raine's THE YUKON TRAIL, Charles Alden Seltzer's GONE NORTH, Max Brand's TORTURE TRAIL, Luke Short's THE BARREN LAND MURDERS, and Harry Sinclair Drago's THE SNOW PATROL. A handful of others alternated between Westerns and Northern adventure, among them Courtney Riley Cooper, whose END OF STEEL is an eye-opening account of early railroad-building in Alaska, and Frank Richardson Pierce, primarily a pulp fictioneer who produced more than a hundred tales of bush piloting, dog-sledding, and other Far North pursuits, the best of which are contained in his 1950 small-press collection, RUGGED ALASKA STORIES.

Among all the glittering sagas of the North, naturally, were works of an alternative nature. Even such magazines as *North-West Stories,* as well-edited as any pulp, were not above publishing a clunker now and then. The lending-library houses occasionally included Northerns as part of their Western lists, and in fact two LLP regulars furnished several titles each. One was Charles S. Strong, whose Charles Stoddard byline appears on more than a dozen Arcadia House, Dodge, Gateway, and Phoenix Press Northerns (most of which, despite melodramatic prose, have an authentic and entertaining flavor); the other was Samuel Alexander White, a Phoenix mainstay in the '30s and early '40s, whose work has a distinctively alternative flavor. The redoubtable Archie Joscelyn tried his hand at a Northern at least once. And in England, there were a number of homegrown scriveners of varying degrees of alternative merit.

The percentage of quality-challenged Northerns, however, is much lower than that among traditional Westerns, perhaps because the specialized knowledge required to write one convincingly enough for publication deterred those who not only preferred conventional tales of hoofbeats and blazing sixguns but could write them with no more research than could be found in a jug of coffin varnish. Still, the dedicated prospector can find enough gold to justify a short chapter such as this one.

We'll commence with THE FROZEN TRAIL, a rousing 1924 saga of "the wild Klondike, the rough Northern adventurers, the Northwest Mounted Police, the snow and mountain peaks...all combined into a book of action, written with all the untamed vigor of the country which it depicts," according to the dust-jacket blurb. The author was British thriller and adventure writer Austin J. Small, who is best known for such lurid mystery/horror tales—published under his own name and the pseudonym Seamark—as THE MAN THEY COULDN'T ARREST, THE DEATH MAKER, and THE AVENGING RAY. THE FROZEN TRAIL appears to have been his only novel of the snowy wastes, though he did perpetrate a number of

Northern shorts, some of which can be found in posthumous Seamark collections published in the '30s.

What makes this novel alternative, aside from the highly improbable adventures it chronicles, is the rather strange and hot-blooded dialogue that issues from heroes and villains alike. No noose-dodger in any other Northern sounds quite like Bully Magain, leader of a gang of vicious river rats who terrorize the good citizens of Cedar Falls, Yukon Territory:

> "Gentlemen, I'm the lord of creation! Did you know that? Well, I'm telling you. I'm the lord high Boss of the Universe and I'm coming round in a minute to pull all your noses. You ought to be proud of it. Tain't often I find time to call around on Cedar Falls, but when I do, I guess I do the honours proper. And in acknowledgment of same, Cedar Falls is going to lick my boots!"

> "Hey! you babes and suckers, I'm Bully Magain, I am! I'm first cousin to a bull buffalo. I'm the toughest, roughest, cussedest cuss on the whole blamed line River! I'm the li'l' feller that keeps the Canadian Mounted on the jump! I eat bear meat raw! Hear that, you swabs? I take my meat warm off the bone. I'm a fighter, I am— and…I'll learn you half-suckled no-goods what it means to wear man clothes in a man country!"

One of Bully's henchmen, Coldwater Griff, is no less gnarly, even when he's talking to the Boss of the Universe himself:

> "Aw! you make me tired!" he growled. "You're one of them unbelievin' Jews who won't believe your own darn death till yeh spook crawls out'n yeh body and shins down the tree to get a ground-floor view of its corpsy [sic] danglin' on a branch!"

Nor has any Northern hero ever slung words in quite the same way as Robert Endersley, gold hunter, lover, and all-around skookum he-wolf. Here he is, speaking first to Bull Magain in a barroom showdown—

> "You're the ugliest, nastiest, least-useful swab that ever hit Creation. The Devil himself got up with a liver the day you were born. If sin was coloured, you'd look pickled. The earth will heave a sigh of relief the day you go back into it. Wherever you die, your grave will

be a standing insult to the country you are buried in. For three pins
I'd push the nose clean off you."

—and later to his lady love, June Royal, who is engaged in beating
the crap out of Coldwater Griff with a whip after Endersley, weak
and wounded, had "shot his bolt" by hurling some flower pots at
Griff, "the shock and sudden demonical exertion" of which "had
set up a chaotic twitching of muscles and tendons long since
fallen into the coma of desuetude":

> "Soak him, lassie! Take the hide off him! Give him what he's given
> Nell, whoever she is; give him what he was going to give you! Sock
> into him, lassie; cut him up; pickle him! Gee! You're the greatest he-
> girl that ever breathed!"

🐎 🐎 🐎 🐎

As hard-boiled as are Bull Magain and Coldwater Griff, they
can't hold a hogleg to the villain who lopes through the pages of
THE BULL MOOSE, a 1931 masterpiece by Ridgwell Cullum. Another
Brit who penned several Far North tales—HOUND OF THE NORTH,
CHILD OF THE NORTH, THE WOLF PACK, THE MYSTERY OF THE BARREN
LANDS are some of the others—Cullum is probably best known for
THE VAMPIRE OF N'GOBI, a well-regarded fantasy/horror tale set in
the African jungle. He seems to have actually visited the Canadian
wilderness, since his settings not only are elaborately described
but have the ring of authenticity; but when it came to devising a
believable story, he often fell short of the mark. In THE BULL
MOOSE he fell so far short he couldn't have found the mark with a
company of Cree Indian trackers.

The featured players in this Northland epic are a tough prospector, Jim McBarr; his "granite-hard Scottish dame," one Marthe,
who is reputed to be "as soulless as a bank without its honesty";
their illegitimate son, 20-year-old Sandy; Wanita, a beautiful half-
breed (who is "charmingly naked" when we first meet her); Inspector Jack Danvers of the Northwest Mounted Police; Scut Barber, a
shrewd drunk who one night "surprised his blankets with a wholly
sober body"; and Faro Neale, a "hard-shell gunman" and gambler,

whose "manhood was rather magnificent" and whose philosophy of life is, "It's no sort o' use blinkin' things. If you're huntin' dollars it's a full-time game that don't leave you play time fer sweatin' around."

The setting is the Kaska Indian country and the Valley of the Moose, through which runs the gold-rich Alikine River and in which is Reliance, a "derelict old fur post hundreds of miles from any living soul with a spot of civilization in them." Rebuilt by Marthe into a great store, the old post is surrounded by "a dump of shacks and dugouts they call a town."

Sandy and Wanita are in love, but Jim McBarr doesn't want them to get hitched. As he counsels Sandy in his warm, fatherly fashion:

> "If you marry Wanita you can forget Marthe and me ever bred you and raised you. You can't mix color in the human body without producing the sort of stuff that belongs to a red hot hell. It's against nature; it's against life. A bitch wolf and a dog father can't sport better than a cur malemute."

It's not that old Jim is prejudiced against Indians or half-breeds or any other nonwhite; no, it's just that he's a Scot and Marthe's a Scot, and, well, "I'd still have to be me if you were a black from Africa and Marthe was a yellow Chink."

Sandy, however, is determined to have Wanita. Jim and Marthe are determined to stop him from having her. Faro Neale is determined to have Wanita, too, one way or another. Scut Barber is determined to get rich so he can stay drunk and disappoint his blankets. Sandy is determined to avenge the brutal murder of Wanita's parents by the Bull Moose, scourge of the Kaska Indian country and the Valley of the Moose. Inspector Danvers of the NWMP is determined to bring the Bull Moose to justice. And the Bull Moose is determined to keep on being an at-large scourge. All of which determination makes for plenty of exciting conflict, as you can well imagine.

Just who is the Bull Moose? Why, he's a killer, a rogue supreme, a scourge among scourges. As Danvers explains to a superior officer from Ottawa:

> "If you went up to Reliance and asked them you'd hear of a bogey
> they regard as something almost super-human. You'd hear of a
> queer figure looking something like the whole forequarters of a real
> bull moose. They'd tell you of a big man whose garments are a
> parka of moose fur reaching to his thighs. And of a pair of fur chaps
> reaching to his heels. Then they'd tell you of a headpiece that's
> joined to the neck of the parka, and which is no less than the great
> drooping tines of a fine bull moose, with the original fur mask en-
> tirely concealing the human face beneath it....
>
> "The Bull Moose! They talk of him as if he'd got clean out of the
> pages of a fairy story and come to life."

The Bull Moose's "methods are theatrical," Danvers admits in a
brilliant piece of understatement, but pretty effective just the
same. Up there in the Valley of the Moose, he "has got the whole
four thousand murdering Kaska Indians right in the palms of his
two hands. He's got them hypnotized to do his bidding in just the
way he's hypnotized the folk of Reliance into a sort of superstitious
fear of him." What he and his murdering Kaska Indians do is to
run around robbing prospectors along the gold-rich Alikine River
of all their hard-earned dust, though it is the murdering Kaskas
who do most of the work. Just before the getaway, in Danvers'
words,

> "The Bull Moose suddenly appears out of—nowhere. He's in full
> view of the claim, but at a point that's safe from gunplay. He just
> stands there and looks through his mask with its crazy drooping
> horns. When his victim's seen him there comes a deep imitation of
> a moose's bellow at the rutting season, or a laugh. Then he goes
> ...or just fades away."

Some Moose.

Can't you just see him, running like the wind through the for-
ests of the Valley of the Moose, his great drooping horns flopping,
his wicked eyes gleaming through holes in his moose mask? Can't
you just hear his maniacal laugh, the old moose-on-the-rut laugh,
"the same as if he was calling you a crazy, helpless darn fool who
don't matter anyway"?

Of course, despite what the murdering Kaska Indians and the

superstitious white folk up at Reliance believe, the Bull Moose isn't really a superhuman bogey. No, he's human—a greedy gent whose manhood is rather magnificent, in fact, and who has a philosophy of life remarkably similar to that of a certain hard-shell gunman and gambler. Surprise? No more so to the jaded reader than the fact that Sandy and Wanita turn out to be star-crossed lovers: Wanita fails to survive to the final chapter, which makes Jim and Marthe very happy, even if they aren't really prejudiced, because now she and Sandy won't be sporting up any malemutes.

Here's to the Bull Moose. Long may he lope and flop and rut in the forefront of legendary alternative villains.

★ ★ ★ ★

The writer of Northerns who contributed the most chunks of alternative "yaller stuff" was Samuel Alexander White. Born in a Canadian pioneer village called Buffy, he was the son of naturalist James White. "I spent several years in teaching," he wrote in a 1935 letter to *Adventure*, "but the lure of the mining camps and fur posts proved too strong and I abandoned the schoolroom" to join a Northern Ontario silver rush and "take up the pen." His "literary" career spanned some 40 years; his first novel, STAMPEDER, was published in 1910 and was followed sporadically by 18 others, 10 of which bore the Phoenix Press imprint (1938–45). He was also a frequent supplier of pulp fiction to such magazines as *Adventure, North-West Stories,* and *Complete Northwest Novel.*

In some Phoenix and pulp blurbs he is referred to as the "Jack London of Canada," an appellation which may have been self-inflicted and which not only insults the real Jack London but may well have provoked London's shade into an ectoplasmic rage. There is no question that White had first-hand knowledge of his Canadian-bush backgrounds, and that his long suit was an effective portrayal of these backgrounds, in particular Northern Ontario and the activities of the Hudson's Bay Company in the vicinity of James Bay. There is also no question that, as one Canadian critic has been quoted as saying, "White's books were so disorganized, badly written and inconsistent that it is hard to understand why they were published."

White could write an effective short story now and then, but the plots of his longer works are indeed mishmashes of disconnected scenes peopled by fictional characters who could not possibly have existed anywhere except in his turgid imagination. His novels bulge with cowboys and Canadian frontiersmen named Whipstalk Wes, Bucking Bart, Rider Imp, Diamond-Thumb Jerome, Colonel Butt, Hang-Fire Hallett, Kootenay Kilgour, and Chris the Mex; with Indians named Blowing Soup, Silver Bit Dug, Never Sick Once, Old Blind, and Chief North Axe; and with magnificent steeds known as Plains Burner, Gray Ghost, and Blueballs. He even managed to make such real historical figures as Louis Riel, leader of the Metis separatists, colorless and silly; and to render such dramatic incidents as train robberies, buffalo hunts, the Second Northwest Rebellion, and the French and Indian Uprising in Saskatchewan about as exciting as an in-depth study of navel lint.

The main reason for this was his prose style, which makes a Beadle & Adams dime novel of the 1880s seem positively terse. His descriptive passages, for one thing, are arch and as lavender as Aunt Fanny's lilacs.

> Her hair, wind-rippled, looked like molten sunlight; her blue eyes outflashed the Kansas spring sky; her full, curved cheeks and dainty chin were as bright as the bronze face of a mountain goddess streaking prairieward from the Rockies in the distance. Her slim arms, agile as darting javelins, alternately waved and reined, fluttering the open collared, gray, pearl-buttoned waist that she wore with her chamois-colored riding costume and striking tan boots and copper hued chaps encasing her mobile thighs with whipping jacket tails. (CALLED NORTHWEST)

> Her voice was like the wind of dawn, too, rising from far away, vibrant, vigorous, but at the same time sweet and undoubtedly fragrant, with the rhythm of new things strumming through it, chords in a faint echo from beyond the rose horizon. Her laugh was in harmony, softly voluminous, thrilling and winning, revealing a world of hope and delight in prospect for her in her lustrous youth. (NORTHWEST PATROL)

Ruby Fleury shoved the porch shutters open in her earnest pertur-
bation, the yellow light of the lantern she had picked up painting
her there with a magical brush of ocher and umber. She was tall,
massive, as deep-bosomed as she was deep-voiced. More elderly-
looking than a cousin she loomed, rather like the figure of an aunt.
Had she been black-skinned, she would have been well suited to
the appellation of Auntie Ruby or Mammy Fleury, but she was
white, and her training as a nurse in Civil War days made her scru-
pulously white, hygienic, with a refreshing personal perfume that
suggested the wild fragrance of mountain flowers and the watery
plunge of prairie streams. (CALLED NORTHWEST)

Remarkably stilted dialogue was another of White's alternative
attributes. None of which was actually *said*, you understand, since
he had an aversion to that particular word; his people preferred to
rasp, trill, gurgle, whoop, exclaim, chatter, splutter, grit, chirrup,
chafe, titter, propound, flatter, belittle, blare, squeak, fume, cackle,
elucidate, and coo their words. They are constantly cackling and
cooing such dubious phrases as "By all the gum-shoed ginks of
detectives" and "Let's call a spade a son-of-a-shovel," and gurgling
such remarkable passages as:

"Gosh golly, Aunt Flo," he burst out, "they sure have made it somehow. Those shots and Peter the Greek's yowl in the middle of that
Metropolitan Opera rendition of his, quaked me for one dizzy minute. But don't worry, I'll pull out of it. I've had those spells before
now—hold-ups and ambushing Injun war parties and such trifling
trail incidents." (NORTHWEST LAW)

"Told you I'd duck you in the Marsh Mallow if you stuck your nose
in here once more...and that's where you're sliding so greasily now,
Major Wade. Isn't far across the valley bottleneck. Smell the swamp
water? Sniffs better than Kentucky whiskey in the spring, eh, Colonel Butt?"

"Condemn you, Kansas cuss," gritted the Major. (CALLED
NORTHWEST)

"You see, we're not standing on ceremony here," she told him.
"We're in camp, on the prairie, in the open, away from everything.
Politeness, manner of address, the way we meet—well, it just
comes naturally, and our words may as well be the same. You don't

mind, do you?"

"Charmed with a charm deeper than snake charm," joked Bob.
(NORTHWEST PATROL)

"Look out," she exclaimed, "look out! You're upsetting the table.
You're spilling the coffee, too. There it goes!"

The lunch table crashed down to Court's swift, secret knee push.

The coffee cups crashed off the tray as he slanted the tray into
Constable Slade's lap where he sat so hungrily....

The Constable exploded into crisp speech.

"Heavens! hold hard, waiter. You've handed me out a scalding."
(NORTHWEST LAW)

Heavens! Hold hard, reader. I have handed you out another alternative classic. Yes, and more to charm you with a charm deeper
than snake charm are yet to come.

The tall tall-man and Clay Thompson turned toward the inter-ruption. Up the middle of the empty street it came. It walked like a man but it was different. There was always something different about a professional gunfighter walking to a gunfight.

The strong face of the tall tall-man of death went stronger. His eyes narrowed on the challenger, blazing as savage as those of a black cat on Hallowe'en. His voice broke loose from his throat like the devil rasping in a graveyard at midnight. "You've made a fool play, mister."

"We'll see!" snarled the antagonist. His hand swooped to his side. He saw in that instant the golden flames of one of The Big Gun's forty-fives screaming toward him and he fell to the ground. He was dead when he got there.—John Fonville, WHERE THE BIG GUN RIDES

5. Paperback Follies; or, "I Don't Care If I Go Crazy..."

The American paperback original was born, along with a lot of other "illegitimate" infants, during the Second World War. It only achieved legitimacy many years later, while in its teens, after a prosperous but much-maligned childhood that may or may not have left it permanently traumatized. And it was in its 20s before it threw off the onus of "second-class citizen." But by then it had already taken sweet revenge by fathering a couple of little bastards of its own: the softcore-sex paperbacks of the '60s and '70s (see Chapter 8 for a close-up look at those little bastards in Western garb).

Until World War II, nearly all book-length fiction first appeared between hard covers or as serials in magazines. (Dime novels, which prospered in the 1800s and in the early years of this century, were not so much books as pulp magazines in book form.) A large number of the more successful hard-back mysteries, Westerns, and general novels from 1920 onward were gobbled up by the burgeoning paperback industry throughout the '40s. Pocket Books brought out the first major Western reprint, of William MacLeod

Raine's OH, YOU TEX!, in 1940; Popular Library, Dell, Avon, Bantam, and Handi-Books also issued sagebrush reprints during that decade. As did a handful of small houses that specialized in digest-size abridgments of lending-library books under a variety of imprints, among them Hillman Periodicals (Western Novel Classic, Western Novel of the Month, Fighting Western Novel, Gunfire Western Novel), Crestwood Publications (Black Cat Western, Prize Western Novel), and Century Publications (Century Western).

The first novels written specifically for the paperback market were Green Publishing Company's Vulcan Books line of mysteries, which began in 1944 and lasted through 20 titles into 1946. But it was not until 1950 that the first brand-new soft-cover Western appeared, when Fawcett Publications launched its innovative Gold Medal line of original, male-oriented category novels. When the first batch of Gold Medal books was published in late 1949 and early 1950, editors Richard Carroll and Bill Lengel had already assembled (and would continue to assemble throughout the '50s) a stable of some of the best popular writers of the period by paying royalty advances on the number of copies printed, rather than on the projected number of copies that would be sold; thus writers received handsome initial payments, up to four times as much as hard-cover publishers were paying. And instead of printing hundreds of thousands of copies of a small number of titles, Fawcett sanctioned hundreds of thousands of copies of many titles in order to reach every possible outlet and buyer. This resulted in million-copy sales through several printings of dozens of Gold Medal novels, particularly by such writers as John D. MacDonald and Richard S. Prather in the early '50s.

The "name" author commissioned by Carroll and Lengel to produce the first Gold Medal Western was W. R. Burnett. STRETCH DAWSON, a novelization of Burnett's screenplay for the 1949 Gregory Peck film, *Yellow Sky,* appeared in March of 1950 as the seventh Gold Medal book. It was followed that year by three other Old West yarns by established writers: Les Savage, Jr.'s THE WILD HORSE, Will F. Jenkins' movie tie-in, DALLAS, and William Heuman's GUNS AT BROKEN BOW. Scores more historical and traditional Westerns appeared under the Gold Medal imprint over the next 15 years by such well-regarded individuals as Louis L'Amour, Luke Short, Richard Jessup, Clifton Adams, and Steve Frazee.

The sensation caused by Fawcett's new line led reprint houses such as Avon, Dell, Popular Library, Bantam, and New American Library (Signet) to begin bringing out originals of their own; it also spawned several new publishing ventures that either emphasized originals or published them exclusively: Lion, Ballantine, Pyramid, Graphic, Monarch, and Ace, among others.

Of all the publishers producing originals in the '50s, the one of most interest to the alternative prospector is Donald Wollheim's Ace Books and its line of Double Novels. These glorious postpulp Westerns, mysteries, and science-fiction yarns came two to a package, back to back, and bound so that the half you weren't reading was upside down: "turn this book over for a second complete novel." The early Ace Doubles featured one reprint and one original, but it wasn't long before most volumes contained two ripe new works.

Between 1952 and 1974 nearly 200 Western originals saw print in the Ace Double format (and dozens more of what were considered better-quality items were published as Ace Singles). A small percentage was penned—in many cases, ill-advisedly—by established writers in the field: Louis L'Amour (early works under his own name and the pseudonym Jim Mayo), Frank Gruber, Harry Whittington, Philip Ketchum, Lewis Patten, Brian Garfield (as Brian Wynne and Frank Wynne), Nelson Nye, Louis Trimble, Samuel Anthony Peebles (Brad Ward), and Merle Constiner. The rest sprang from the skewed imaginations of such alternative masters as Walker A. Tompkins, Archie Joscelyn, and Leslie Scott, and such alternative-leaning tale-tellers as J. Edward Leithead, Tom West, Lee Floren, Walt Coburn, Burt Arthur (Herbert Shappiro), Edwin Booth, and Gene Tuttle.

Despite Ace's predilection for pulp-style bang-bangers, and the alternative nature of many of the ones that carried its logo, it somehow failed to produce a single Western that even approaches the classic status of that towering Ace Double mystery, Michael

Morgan's DECOY. The closest to a Hall-of-Famer is probably the very first Ace Double Western original—J. Edward Leithead's BLOODY HOOFS (Ace D–2, bound together with a reprint of William Colt MacDonald's BAD MAN'S RETURN).

Cover-blurbed "A square-shooting wrangler is caught in the crossfire of a no-quarter range war," this bullet-studded cowpatty is set in a drought-ridden corner of West Texas and features the efforts of a drifting waddy named Bret Kane to settle a "bloody triple showdown" among three strong-willed ranchers "who hated each other's guts and itched to pull triggers." Before he succeeds, he must survive a series of "bullet tornadoes" that include a midnight massacre, a desperate flight from a sheriff's posse, a sort of rodeo run by horse thieves, and a last-ditch battle at a "lost" desert waterhole.

According to Ace's editorial blurb-writer, "J. Edward Leithead, veteran author of fast-action Westerns [i.e. '20s-style pulp gunsmokers of the Chuck Martin and Ed Earl Repp ilk], has packed BLOODY HOOFS with more excitement than you'll find in many a long time." Leithead packed it with more creaky prose than you'll find in many a long time, too. The story fairly bulges with such passages as:

> "Word from Bob at last!" the old-timer exclaimed, his chin coming up, his shoulders straightening. With a new light in his cavernous eyes, which was foredoomed shortly to go out again when the nature of Kane's errand was divulged, One-shot Lowrie swung wide the screen door.
>
> In a living room that showed neglect, Bret Kane set himself to the distasteful task of informing the suddenly eager old man that the absent son for whom he was eating his heart out would never come home. Bret, momentarily tongue-tied from the deepest sympathy he had ever felt for a fellow human being, bethought him of the contents of the gunny sack he toted, which might mutely substitute for the words he couldn't bring himself to utter.

🐎 🐎 🐎 🐎

As many quality-free originals as were published in the '50s and early '60s, it was not until 1964 that the first great, nonerotic alternative paperback Western blazed into print. Ironically, even though John Fonville's WHERE THE BIG GUN RIDES is about as sexy as a hooker's daydream, it was published by a notorious sex-book outfit that grew out of the fertile soil of California's Central Valley (headquartered in Fresno and in nearby Clovis) and thrived like ragweed in the late '50s and early '60s. This entrepreneurial bunch specialized in steamy erotica under a number of imprints—Fabian, Saber, Tropic Books.

In 1961, in an effort to (a) honestly expand its none-too-steady empire, or (b) create a protective coloration of legitimacy so as to stave off pressure from public-decency watchdogs, the publishers launched two new lines of traditional genre novels, Suspense Library and Western Library, both under the imprint of Vega Books. Titles in these new lines had very little sexual content. Unfortunately for their sponsors, they also had very little quality content. In large part this dearth of merit can be traced to a disinclination to pay writers other than rock-bottom royalties, so that most novels purchased for the new lines were either commissioned from the company's stable of sex-book hacks or bought from rank amateurs. Even so, a few readable crime stories crept into Vega's Suspense Library, notably two early efforts by mystery and young-adult novelist Willo Davis Roberts, and an above-average Mickey Spillane pastiche by Ennis Willie called VICE TOWN.

The same claim cannot be made of the Western Library. The only near-worthwhile titles therein are a pair of minor Nelson Nye reprints, FRONTIER SCOUT and COME A-SMOKIN'; the other 13 are horse apples. Twelve little horse apples by the likes of Wade Pierce, John Nemec, William Cuthburt, Arthur A. Howe, Allen Stark, Marvin Tuma, and Benny Runnels. And John Fonville's one boulder-size horse apple, WHERE THE BIG GUN RIDES.

The dual heroes of this gutbuster are a mild-mannered bountyhunter (one word, not two, in Fonville's fictional landscape) named Clay Thompson, who is also known as the Baron of the Bountyhunters, and a gunslinger, John William Prince, who is "equally known as" The Big Gun, The Big Gun from Texas, Black Eagle, Mr. Death, the tall tall-man, the tall tall-man of death, the famed giant of mystery, and the loudest living legend of the frontier man's game of the gun.

Clay Thompson doesn't much like being a bountyhunter; he wants to settle down with a good woman in a good town and become a star-toter. The tall tall-man doesn't much like being Mr. Death, either. In fact, he turned into The Big Gun from Texas because he became disillusioned by his experiences fighting for the Union in the Civil War and then found a new life on the Big River, equally known as the Mississippi, where he gambled and drank and "picked up another trait that would later help to romanticize his name across the entire frontier. He found that women loved him. And he simply took the lovely course of least resistance. He loved them back." Then he was forced to start killing scum who tried to make a name for themselves by killing him, which made him even more tired and disillusioned, and now he's heading west to San Francisco where he hopes to quit being a "notorious head-hunter" and settle down with a good woman or maybe a bad one, whichever comes first.

But what Prince *really* wants, as is pointed out to him during a meeting in an abandoned church with a couple of spiritual old folks who are on their way to visit "grand-younguns" in the town of Headstone, which is near Lordsburg in New Mexico Territory ...what he *really* wants is to learn how to whistle a hymn, which is to say make peace with himself and start living a righteous life. But he can't do that as long as scum keep trying to salivate him and he's forced to salivate them instead, because a "big-time killer" isn't fit to whistle a hymn or do much of anything except continue his lonely life of drifting and salivating.

Mr. Death's plight and skill are vividly illustrated for the reader in the very first chapter, which takes place in a ghostly graveyard "somewhere after midnight and before dawn [where] almost human mists of dust dance wildly around jagged rows of tombstones, those bold, vivid markers of death, as if the souls of this eternal underground hotel had risen to play." Enter a seeming giant, who "waited over the dead for death." But not for long: "From its safe distance the moon still watched. And it saw in its own

vague light the hulk of another seeming giant warily enter the
home of the late."

Each seeming giant grows aware of the other's presence. Long
coats are pushed back over lean hips to reveal the "dueling weap-
ons of the day," which Fonville tells us are "Frontier cold [sic]
forty-fives, the steel judges of a raw land, each with a six-count
jury of unconscienced lead." The two men walk toward each other,
slowly. And then—

> The snail-pace march ended and the bullet-pace battle began. It
> was short and to the point. Hot yellow streaked from the flashing
> gun of the giant who had entered the graveyard second. And the
> first man joined the ranks of permanent sleepers. The raging ech-
> oes of six-gun justiced hell died with him.
>
> "You can't win 'em all, mister," arose a voice that you might ex-
> pect to arise from the remaining giant. For the man who had been
> left standing was not just a tall man but a tall tall-man. And his
> voice was as deep as his stature was high.
>
> A light flickered and lit a big cigar in his great face. It was a rug-
> ged face, the face of The Big Gun. Everyone west of the Big River
> knew of the great face of The Big Gun. He was a legend, the loudest
> living legend of the frontier man's game of the gun...and the fron-
> tier woman's game of the heart....
>
> The famed giant of mystery, snorting smoke like a conquering
> dragon of old, turned and strode from the yard of the dead.

Now *that's* a gunfighter! Billy the Kid, John Wesley Hardin? Bah.
I'll take the smoke-snorting, famed giant of mystery any day.

Well, Prince and Clay Thompson soon meet and strike up an
uneasy rapport, after which Black Eagle is forced to bump off
more scum in fair fights, including some local gundogs called the
Slinger brothers who have bounties on their heads. Once the
Slingers have been salivated, Prince surrenders to the Baron of the
Bountyhunters so he, The Big Gun, can have help in salivating all
the other fame-seeking scum who are sure to try pumping the tall
tall-man full of lead, it being the code of the bountyhunter, or the
code of the mild-mannered Baron of the Bountyhunters anyway,
to keep a prisoner alive, for "a man of honor never refuses an obli-
gation of his trade."

So then the Baron and Mr. Death leave town, but not alone; accompanying them is Katie Slinger, beautiful young sister of the gunned Slingers, who is everything her brothers weren't, which is to say she's good and sweet and kind and loving, and Clay has fallen head over spurs for her. She's the girl of his dreams, the one he wants to take as his wife so he can settle down and quit the bountyhunting racket and become an honest and forthright star-toter.

Not long after the trio arrives in Headstone (yes, the very same Headstone, near Lordsburg in New Mexico Territory, to which the spiritual old couple who counseled Prince were bound), the tall tall-man and the mild-mannered one collect the bounty on the Slinger brothers, which Clay generously offers to share with The Big Gun, and then The Big Gun decides to get laid. Of course, he'd rather have the deep and abiding love of "a real little lady" like Katie so he can learn how to whistle a hymn, for after all he "liked they-lived-happily-ever-after stories, especially out of books," but since he doesn't have a real little lady, "a painted one was all his frantic life could afford at the moment." So he picks up a saloon babe and makes arrangements to meet her in her room. After consuming a quart of whiskey, he goes upstairs, enters the room, and sees that the girl is lying face down with a thin nightgown covering her body and her face hidden in the pillows.

> "Playin' asleep," whispered Prince to himself. "And her eyes in the pillows. Such sweet modesty while I shuck out of my clothes."
>
> He undressed quickly and sat on the edge of the bed by the resting beauty. She was lying on her front side with her back side confronting the hungrying Big Gun.
>
> "Honey!" he sighed. "Honey!"
>
> The girl didn't move. Well, asleep or not asleep, he determined to be a touch fresh with a fresh touch. He brushed the flimsy gown up and over a beaming white seat and planted his hand firmly across the naked rear in the manner of a playful slap.
>
> With the resounding "splat" a romantic end upended. A horrifying yelp accompanied the flipping form. The nightgown went down in one hand and the covers up in the other. The yelp became a yell. And the yell became a scream.

"Good Lord, have mercy!" moaned the suddenly sober Big Gun as he stared in the shrieks from a completely strange face. "I'm in the wrong goddamned room!"

While Mr. Death is experiencing one of life's embarrassing moments, Clay and Katie are enjoying a much more romantic tête-à- tête under the benevolent light of a full moon.

Clay put his head down beside that of his goddess. And together, they looked at the moon. The romantic moon.

Then, gradually, they weren't watching the moon. But the moon was still watching them. The romantic moon wouldn't miss this for the world. And the faint light from the heavenly window-peeker graced the pillow of lovers as their lips met.

But the heaven's glowing symbol of romance was to be left hanging. Yet, maybe it was more proud than disappointed. For there is a certain kind of love that expresses itself far deeper than in physical satisfaction. And it was in an innocent closeness of respect that these two young people spent the night.

But enough of chucklesome embarrassing moments and heavenly window-peekers. Back to the salivating.

Prince and Clay face their biggest challenge in Headstone, which is under the cruel thumbs of the Martin brothers—Rake, Mule, Kale, and Wes—and their gaggle of scummy gunslingers. Only Sheriff Tom Courtland and a handful of deputies stand between the Martins and a takeover of Headstone and all that is good and honest and right and true. Naturally the Baron of the Bountyhunters and the loudest living legend of the frontier man's game of the gun must do the right thing and join forces with the law.

And Prince is rewarded for this noble gesture when he meets and falls instantly in love with beautiful young Lucy, who happens to be Rake Martin's girl, but not by choice and never in the Biblical sense, she being good and sweet and kind and loving like Katie Slinger. Lucy's the girl of The Big Gun's dreams. She's the girl who can and will make him hang up his Frontier cold forty-fives and then teach him how to whistle a hymn. If, that is, he survives the murderous intentions of the Martins, who are also known as the

Mad Dogs of Headstone.

The action comes fast and furious at this juncture. There are more gun duels. There is even hand-to-hand combat between Clay and Prince, the result of a disagreement on how best to deal with the Mad Dogs—

> The right hand of the tall tall-man gripped itself. It gave away his plan. As Prince turned back with his powerful arm unleashing the balled fist toward Clay's chin, the bountyhunter was already in action. His own right hand smashed full into the great face with the result of terrible distortion....
>
> The lawmen dismounted to break the furious twosome. But they were too late. They were already in the midst of breaking. And rather colorfully. Clay had been hoisted high by Prince and was now sailing through the air like something that had not yet been invented. When he landed, it was his turn to be dazed. He was aware that The Big Gun was hovering over him and even more aware that he was hovering at the top of his voice.

The final gun battle between the forces of good and evil is of epic proportions, told in brilliant metaphor:

> The Big Gun took to the street. And he was walking. Walking for the end of it and the Martins. Walking slow and steady. Walking for a town. Walking for life. Walking for death. Walking. The tall tall-man was walking....
>
> The time for lip talk was past. The time for gun talk was present. And the mouth of a six-gun screamed. It was that of John William Prince that had the first word....
>
> The six-guns of Wes and Kale shouted simultaneously with Prince's second explosion. The cold heart of Wes Martin was to grow a lot colder. But at the moment it was bursting and burning. The Big Gun's oratory had hit peak performance. No shot thrown by any frontier pistol had ever been truer to its mark or brought faster results. Wes Martin was dead on his feet and his fall was inconsequential.
>
> Kale Martin never fired again. Ever. Prince's fire and brimstone sermon had risen to a thundering height and he was rending his agitators speechless. Kale gagged and staggered at the third flaming and booming point of that furious lecture.

As stimulating as the foregoing is, Fonville and The Big Gun save their all-out best for the demise of Rake Martin, the slavering head of the Mad Dog pack:

> Rake Martin was to make one final attempt at regaining his suddenly lost status as a true fighter. His whining ceased. And his weapon began to slowly rise from the dry dust of dismal defeat into the gun-smoked air of potential victory. The air of war. That same challenging air of death that has labeled heroes and cowards throughout the history of man. For the male child grows from the crib in an obligation of manhood. The choice of good and evil is his. But the responsibility of the sex is predestined. And it was with the full knowledge of this responsibility that the lost Rake Martin was trying to die as a man.
>
> Prince was fully aware of the struggle before him. The barrel of the gun continued to rise in his direction. And he waited. But why was he waiting? Had he come this far to search for death? Was he once again defying all odds and making the end of his own trail? Had he tired of his wild ride on the great horse of life? Was he dismounting forever?

Nah. He quits asking himself rhetorical questions and salivates the Dog right between the eyes.

And then he takes another walk, whistling as he goes. Whistling a hymn at long last. Whistling "When the Roll Is Called Up Yonder, I'll Be There."

Finis.

But before we leave the mild-mannered Baron and the tall tallman, I can't resist quoting a few more passages from this one-of-a-kind leather-slapper. In addition to Fonville's other alternative attributes, he had a rare talent for devising the pithy said substitute:

> "He's done it!" fanged out Rake.

> "That son of a bitch is crazy!" heehawed Mule.

> "You goddamned right we got you!" iced Wes.

> "Ain't nobody can whip me!" Mule loudly claimed his chief claim to fame.

> "He's my prisoner, sheriff," rumbled Prince-thunder.

And he could mangle the English language in ways that invite exclamations of "Huh?" as well as chuckles.

Every person on that street was staring at the suddenly changed Rake Martin and his way-too-big smile, while the sadistic sound of the wind groaned over his sarcasm.

Livid red streaks were obvious across each of his cheeks. The marks from Clay's vicious slaps blended symbolically into the crazed expression of revenge carved on his face.

Prince swept back his coat tails and placed his hands on the two angry-looking pistols at his sides. The quiet fear that gripped the room suddenly became a quieter panic. Clay innately went to a [gun] drawing position.

Mule Martin's bullyishness was apparent in his whole demeanor.

Clay's actions since the poker game at dawn had bred their consequences. And those consequences were coming to a head outside.

There was a long pause in the [verbal] sparring. One thing for sure was in every mind on that street. Tom Courtland was a talking man. And he didn't just talk words. He talked thoughts. And his thoughts were well worth thinking about no matter in whose head they were.

🐎 🐎 🐎 🐎

In 1966 one of the bottom-end paperback houses, Belmont Books, launched a short-lived series of "Two Double-Barreled Westerns" per book, after the fashion of Ace Doubles. There were three differences in the Belmont versions: The "novels" were much shorter than Ace's, well under 40,000 words each; they were bound one after the other rather than one upside down; and they shared a split front cover instead of each having a cover of its own. Most of the Belmont doubles seem to have been originals, though some may well be unattributed reprints of pulp novellas.

Like the bulk of Ace Double Westerns, Belmont's were tried and true bang-bangers. E. B. Mann, a moderately well regarded action writer in the '30s and early '40s, was responsible for nearly a dozen titles, two thirds of the total number of "Double-Barreled Westerns" published between 1966 and 1968. Others were written by

Burt Arthur, Lee Floren, and the one-time "King of the Cowboy Writers," Walt Coburn.

Easily the worst of the Belmont crop—a chunk of Yellow Peril nonsense in Western dress called BORDER TOWN—was the drooling brainchild of Coburn, perhaps devised early in his career when he was still learning his trade, or concocted out of liquor-soaked whole cloth near the end of his rather tempestuous life. It is unclear whether this 30,000-word deformity is a pulp reprint or an original.

Like Chuck Martin, Tom Roan, and other legendary crankers, Walt Coburn enjoyed both a long and a commendably prolific career. Between 1922 and 1970 he published upwards of a thousand pieces of short Western fiction and nonfiction in *Argosy, Adventure, Western Story, Lariat, Dime Western, True West, Frontier Times,* and dozens of other magazines; close to a hundred novels; and a couple of acclaimed histories of cowboy and ranching life in his native Montana. He was the only Western writer other than Zane Grey to have more than one magazine named after him: *Walt Coburn's Action Novels,* a Fiction House publication that ran briefly in 1931, featured four of his cowboy novelettes per issue, and carried a Will Rogers quote ("I read all of Walt Coburn's stories") on the cover; and *Walt Coburn's Western Magazine,* a Popular Publications pulp in 1949–50 that in each issue contained one long Coburn novelette, and one nonfiction reminiscence under the umbrella title "Walt's Tally Book."

During his heyday in the '30s and '40s, Coburn churned out an average of 600,000 words of Western pulp per year. (His total published wordage, by his own estimate, was nearly 20 million words.) "In all my years of fiction writing," he claimed in his posthumously published autobiography, WALT COBURN, WESTERN WORD WRANGLER (1973), "I never rewrote a story, never missed a deadline, drunk or sober, never used an agent, but dealt directly with editors, and never used a pseudonym." He was a prodigious drinker and allowed as how he worked many times with a bottle of whiskey beside his typewriter. (His autobiography drips with accounts of various wet escapades, a couple of Machiavellian complexity.)

About his pulp writing he stated proudly: "I went after the job as if it were a game from which I got a big kick. I had no set plan of work, no idea in my head, just a kind of cockeyed, haphazard way of putting down words on paper.... My plots came from the stars. I might awaken in the middle of the night with some idea which would keep me awake. Dreams took shape, the plots just came from nowhere."

Some of Coburn's dreams translated well into fiction; others were thinly disguised nightmares, whiskey-induced or not, which resulted in stories that were downright terrible. BORDER TOWN is one such nightmare. If its plot "came from the stars," it was a mischievous alien presence that transmitted it telepathically into Coburn's fevered brain. And he was never more cockeyed or haphazard in putting its words down on innocent sheets of typing paper.

The setting is not the Montana cattle country of much of his Western output, a background he knew intimately and wrote about with authority, but Ensenada and the nearby Mexican wilderness. The time is the flapper era, circa 1925. Herbert Smith, a.k.a. Dick Smith, an American remittance man hooked on booze and marijuana, "the Mexican substitute for opium," is hanging out in his usual haunt, a squalid cantina in Ensenada's Chinese sector (?) run by Quo Wong, "a slant-eyed, close tongued half-caste" who is also an expert knife-thrower. Herb–Dick begins beating up on Rosita, his bar-girl enamorata because she won't give him any more "hop." Enter then a lean, tough Texan named Jones who proceeds to abuse the abuser, and for his trouble almost gets a knife in the neck.

No sooner is order restored than another American, a criminal attorney named Crittenden Briggs, a close pal of Herb–Dick's millionaire industrialist father, shows up and spirits the Texan away to a better-quality watering hole for some private palaver. Briggs has a scheme: He wants Jones to kidnap Herb–Dick and spirit *him* off into the wilderness, where with the help of a faithful old Chinese retainer, one Ah Hell, Jones will spend a year breaking Herb–Dick of his drug habit. At the end of that year, Jones, if he is successful, will receive $10,000 and Herb–Dick will be allowed to claim a large inheritance from his father. Jones refuses at first, but Briggs has some dirt on him and, with the added promise of $10,000 for his troubles, talks Jones into going along with the plan.

So the Texan, with the aid of a touring car and its driver, Hans, kidnaps Herb–Dick and transports him to a camp in the rock-strewn hills where Ah Hell awaits. But not before he, Jones, barely manages to escape the clutches of Weasel Stanley, an implacable "human ferret"—a sort of Lieutenant Girard prototype—who has chased Jones halfway around the world so as to arrest him on a charge of bank robbery.

Okay. That's the general setup. So now you think you have a pretty fair idea of how the rest of the plot develops, right?

Well, you're wrong.

You're wrong because what I've just outlined to you is almost entirely illusion and red-herring and brainless motivation and pure crap. Very little of the early setup and none of the characters are exactly what they seem to be.

Herb–Dick Smith is really a World War I draft-dodger named Herbert Freuling, son of a rich Bosch sympathizer named August Freuling.

Jones is really Zack Davis, who is neither a Texan nor a bank robber (and not much of a hero, either), though he is a fugitive from a trumped-up bank-robbery charge.

Quo Wong is not a sleazy, half-witted bar owner; he's the cunning head of a ring smuggling Chinese across the border into the U.S., *and* the Oxford-educated son of an English lord who was thrown out of England for taking a Chinese wife. He says things like "If you have got the wrong line of information on this, old dear, it'll go bloody well hard with you. I am much upset over the loss of our dear old Herb, you know. Quite upset. Damnably so."

Rosita is neither a simple Mexican bar-girl nor Herb–Dick's love interest, but a refugee from Los Angeles who likes to dress in clothing "copied from Hollywood fashions as set by the moving picture folk," is in the employ of Quo Wong, and speaks thusly: "The Hans hombre had on a crying jag and when I pet him ever so

little, and let the big fish hold my hand, he spill the beans, no
foolin', and tell about the way this smart jane gets a bird to liquor
him all up, see."

The Hans hombre, driver of the kidnap touring car, is neither
Hans nor an hombre; she is really a beautiful girl named Billy who
may or may not be in love with Herb–Dick Smith–Frueling, may or
may not be engaged to marry Herb–Dick, and may or may not
have an ulterior motive for jumping off August Freuling's yacht in
the Ensenada harbor and then knocking out the real Hans and
dressing up in his clothing and joining up with Zack Davis–Jones
and Ah Hell in the effort to help Herb–Dick kick his booze-and-
hop habit.

Ah Hell is not a faithful family retainer but a cohort of Quo
Wong, except that he really *isn't* working for Quo Wong but has
murkier motives that have to do with hating the Bosch sympathizer and his draft-dodging son and not wanting Herb–Dick to
kick the hooch-and-drug habit, to which end he secretly supplies
Herb–Dick with booze and hop after Zack and Billy deliver the
young wartime slacker to the camp in the rock-strewn hills. *He*
delivers such lines as "Ketchem bossy-man Herb? Heap good. Too
much Quo Wong Mexican hop, smokum. Blekfas' leady now."

Crittenden Briggs is in fact a "great criminal defender," but he
isn't really in the employ of August Freuling and doesn't really care
about Herb–Dick's welfare; his true interest lies in the fact that he
is secretly Billy's father and doesn't want her to marry a draft-
dodger, drunkard, hop-head, and son of a dirty Bosch sympathizer.

And Weasel Stanley, while a tenacious human ferret, isn't really
such an implacable sort after all but a good old boy who befriends
Zack Davis–Jones, helps him to subdue Herb–Dick when the
young slacker becomes "glassy-eyed with insensate hate" because
his hop supply has been drastically reduced, and then joins forces
with Zack in an effort to thwart Quo Wong and his pack of "yellow-
fanged, grinning celestials."

Confused? Imagine how I felt, reading this mind-altering blather for the first time. Imagine how Walt Coburn must have felt,

writing it with what may have been a large hangover and possibly with numerous nibbles from a fresh jug of whiskey next to his typewriter.

Mercifully condensed, the balance of the narrative amounts to this: Billy is taken prisoner by Quo Wong and Ah Hell, who are heading for their smuggler's hideout in a little town on the edge of El Desierto Arenas. She thinks Zack Davis–Jones is dead, the result of a sneak attack by a murdering compadre of Quo Wong's, but Ah Hell knows that Zack survived the attack and broke the assassin's neck instead, and since Ah Hell is only half bad he flashes her a Morse Code message by means of sun reflections off the blade of his knife to let her know Zack is okay (which, of course, earns him a quick exit when Quo Wong tumbles to what he's doing).

Herb–Dick Smith–Freuling escapes from Zack Davis–Jones and Weasel Stanley, but not before he induces them to give him a desperately needed shot of hooch. ("He pressed the flask to his lips and the metal clinked like a clock against his shaking teeth.") Zack and the human ferret rush in pursuit of the "damned murdering Chinks" who have swiped Billy, and get close enough to spot Ah Hell's Morse Code flashes. ("'Z A K O K,' muttered Stanley. 'Sounds like a hair tonic.'") Herb–Dick also charges off in pursuit of the "filthy half-caste son of an exiled Britisher whose country kicked him out" (Quo Wong) and his "Chink playmates." One of the playmates ambushes Zack and Weasel, and the human ferret is wounded, thus delaying Zack and allowing Herb–Dick to get to Quo Wong and Billy first.

Herb–Dick, in a final effort to atone for his draft-dodging, boozing, and hop-heading, challenges Quo Wong to a Jim Bowie–style duel in which they each take one end of a scarf between their teeth and then try to carve each other up with knives. Which they both manage to do, delivering killing blows at approximately the same instant.

Billy is saved. Zack Davis–Jones rides in anticlimactically (I told you he wasn't much of a hero), just in time to profess his undying love for Billy and to learn that she never really loved Herb–Dick Smith–Freuling but felt sorry for him and hoped to change him and now that he's been filleted by that "yellow devil" Quo Wong, why, she's free to marry Zack whom she fell in love with the first moment she saw him in the kidnap touring car while disguised as Hans. And he's free to marry her because just before the final fade-out he finds out that he has been cleared of the trumped-up bank-robbery charge and no longer has anything to fear from Weasel Stanley or any other human ferret.

And if all of that isn't the ultimate overdose of hop-hooch-and-hair-tonic, I'm not sure I want to be subjected to the "plot from the stars" that outdoes it.

🐎 🐎 🐎 🐎

Over the past quarter-century, a handful of enterprising new publishing houses have made valiant if mostly unsuccessful attempts to compete in the mass-market paperback trade. Only one, Carroll & Graf, has had any persistent success. The most recent of the failed newcomers to sponsor a line of Western originals was Major Books, a poorly distributed and editorially challenged Southern California outfit. During its four-plus years of existence (1975–79), Major published well over a hundred fiction and non-fiction titles with emphasis on category novels—mysteries, spy stories, Gothic romances, science fiction, and Westerns. Among such a large output one would expect to find at least half a dozen books of some quality. Major and its editorial mavens defied the law of averages, however. Only *one* book with any claim to literary merit appeared under the Major imprint: Loren D. Estleman's maiden novel, THE OKLAHOMA PUNK (1976).

Ah, but on the alternative side of the ledger...

Nearly 40 Westerns carried the Major Books logo. A few were early efforts by writers who went on to bigger and better accomplishments in the Western field (Jory Sherman, James Powell); a few more were late-career and trunk items penned by pulpsters and crossover writers (J. L. Bouma, A. A. Baker, Margaret and George Ogan); one was a novelization of a 20-year-old Rory Calhoun flick, *The Domino Kid*, written by none other than Rory Calhoun himself and published as THE MAN FROM PADERA; and the balance are the alternatively gened offspring of wannabes, never-should-have-beens, and never-heard-from-agains (Ladell J. Futch, Dean W. Ballenger, Martin Ryerson, Charles G. Muller, Steve Sherman, Cliff Davis, Charles Plumb).

The plots of most Majors were minor; that is, standard gun-thunderers whose chief ingredient was violence lavishly described, often in stomach-churning detail. Lawmen, owlhooters, waddies, soldiers, Indians, Mexicans, and other traditional frontier fighting folk spill each other's blood in all manner of trite shootouts, raids, skirmishes, and pitched battles. Only one title offers any real departure from the formula. And as luck would have it, that one is Major's major contribution to the Alternative Hall of Fame.

THE CAVES, a snazzy little underground thriller, was the joint effort of Norman Thaddeus Vane and R. Rude. At least, the novel would seem to be a collaboration, since both names appear on it; yet the copyright is in Norman Thaddeus Vane's name alone and on the copyright page there is an odd little disclaimer: "This novel was co-written, but is based on the original story by Norman Thaddeus Vane, who created the original idea and all the characters and dialogue." Hmmm. So just what did R. Rude do to earn a byline credit? Edit the thing? Write passages of narrative to complement Norman Thaddeus's idiosyncratic dialogue? Or did he have something on Norman Thaddeus and take partial credit as a unique form of blackmail payoff? In any case, the impression one gleans from the disclaimer is that Norman Thaddeus wasn't too happy at having to share his glory with somebody named Rude. If Mr. or Ms. Rude was in fact responsible for some of the ruder aspects of the tale, then Norman Thaddeus had every right to be upset.

The story, we are told in a brief forward, is based on historical fact; and the setting, a labyrinth of caves in the Huachuca Mountains of southern Arizona near the Mexican border, not only is a real place but was once a refuge for Geronimo, and "to this day, the way out of the Caves remains an Apache secret." Well, maybe.

The time is May of 1884 and a band of murderous Chiricahua

Apaches led by Geronimo has escaped from the White Mountain Reserve and left a bloody trail of dead civilians and burned-out farms and mine stakes in its wake. In pursuit is the 4th Cavalry out of Fort Huachuca, under the command of Major Emmett Pilcher. A few survivors of the Indian attacks have been picked up by the soldiers and brought along for want of anything better to do with them. Both soldiers and some of the civilian whites are spurred by more than just a desire for justice, revenge, and/or safety: A bounty of $100 in gold for every Apache scalp has been offered by the government.

Hunted and hunters meet at a spot called Skeleton Canyon in the Huachucas. Geronimo and his renegades appear to be trapped; the soldiers and civilians brace for battle. But then the Apaches disappear in the Caves, the secret entrance to which Pilcher and his command soon stumble upon. Should they follow the Indians inside? Yes, and a bad decision it turns out to be: A landslide (triggered by a "freak tornado," no less) kills several of the party and traps 13 others in the maze of subterranean passages. Thus begins, as the back-cover blurb has it, "an incredible two-month odyssey of desperate men set against nature and one another. Terrified soldiers and civilians are faced with Apaches in ambush, death, starvation, and utter despair! The reward that drives them on is no longer gold—it is survival!"

So far so good. All the ingredients are present for a dandy suspense story. In the thorny and none-too-subtle hands of Vane and Rude, however, what develops is an alternative cauldron of super-heated melodrama, brute savagery, and formidably awful prose.

We'll begin with a look at some of the main characters, as described by the authors:

☥ Major Emmett Pilcher: "[His] face was a map of crosscurrents —Scots, Irish, English—tempered badly like impure iron—with the ore of German and Scandinavian blood. The combination seethed, rather than settled in his veins—making him a curiosity of nature—somewhere between a distempered prairie wolf and a bulldog. His Scots' ancestry gave him a rawboned solidity; his Irish and English blood bristled hostility in every instinct.

Reflected in his blue-green eyes was his journeyman's soul. The jaw was too thick, but the lips too full to be a man's man. His big-boned hands and feet were his German curse. His head was topped by a bristle and thistle of carrot-blonde-gray streaked strands of mismatched hair, which compared unfavorably to his horse's."

ϓ Sergeant Talbot: "His shanks of muscle slithered under his shirt threateningly, his gnarled, knotted, calloused fingers aiming [his horse] slipshod among the soldiers. If the major was the devil, Sergeant Talbot was his advocate. Often a sharp slash of whip across a man's or animal's ass made his point."

ϓ Private Orley: "A string of lean meat that ended in a baby face—where two beacons of eyes, blushed in outward innocence. He was from the South, even without opening his mouth, his slink swore it."

ϓ Joshua Barrett, Washington, D.C., newspaper columnist: "Barrett stuck out in the group like a sore, educated thumb. He even looked like a thumb. With his bright, piercing eyes—intelligent eyes—and an always questioning mouth, out of which words tumbled, with a faint ring of contempt."

ϓ Venable Brown, prospector: "[He owned] a wiry mass of hair, which sprouted from his head and face. He was a lead nugget who had spent a lifetime in the fantasy of chasing fool's gold. In his own words, he had found the pot at the end of the rainbow 'was a pissin' pot.'"

ϓ Eli Fly, photographer: "He was a little gnat of a man [with] a gnawed cigar stuck in his goat's face."

ϓ Judge Bedediah Tasker, a.k.a. "Old Necessity": "He drank like a fish, dressed like a deacon, and lived like a gambler. A weasel-faced, slight man, with a perpetual liquor stench, he was a salted product of the West, a drifter and a con man of some repute [who] was once hauled into a saloon in Kansas and made to judge the kangaroo trial of an old Irishman for the killing of a Chinese laborer.... The good judge thumbed through his law books and finally decreed he could find no law that said a Chinaman couldn't be killed in Kansas. Drinks were had by all."

❧ Old Gabe, scalper and bounty hunter: "He had a face like a horned lizard. From a distance he could have been easily mistaken for a barrel cactus. Scalping—after a lifetime of failure—had become a way of life for Gabe. He was an artist, quick and efficient— seven or eight deft strokes and he could lift off the whole top of a head."

❧ Baby Doe Trabber, née Margaret Stallmayer: "Baby Doe was a comely woman in her mid-30s. The sun had not touched her soft, pallid complexion. Her fair skin was an oddity in the dirt-brown desert. She had made marriage her career...had had five marriages and three divorces. [The failure of her last marriage had forced her to] flee from creditors with the last remains of her past splendor, her great fortune, on the back of one jackass."

❧ Bull Whacker, waddy: "A greasy, one-eyed, glass-eyed cowboy, with a face like a tired saddle [who] bristled like a cactus when he was angry [and who] always sided with the man who shouted the loudest."

This truly motley bunch, along with a stoic Indian scout called Dull Knife, a 300-pound black Army cook, and a weathered old farmer cleverly dubbed Sidney Ducks, faces all sorts of wonders, hardships, and terrors while trapped in the Caves. They encounter, not necessarily in order: stalactites, stalagmites, great limestone vaults full of smelly bats, underground streams, sulphur pools brimming with bleached prehistoric fish, human bones, ancient Indian hieroglyphics, deposits of gold, oil, and natural gas, and a cache of fresh and bloody scalps. In addition to Geronimo and his renegade Chiricahuas, they are menaced by a hunger-maddened black bear, falling rocks, razor-sharp stones in a narrow underwater passage they must traverse that are "like jutting teeth whose dangerous edges protruded and scraped them as if they were passing through the gigantic mouth of a swallowing sea monster," and last but far from least, each other when their supplies of food begin to run out. It isn't long before they're forced to eat horses,

mules, bats, green slimy snakes, warty lizards, the prehistoric
bleached fish, and finally—you guessed it—their own dead. Only
a handful of the original group of trapped survivors, naturally,
lasts long enough (and stays sane enough) to chance upon an escape route through an old well in an abandoned churchyard.

All of this is told in a style that ingeniously combines sloppy
syntax, descriptive passages of elaborate incoherence, dialogue
bristling with anachronisms, half-wit wit, and epicurean depic-
tions of various acts of violence and depravity. (The scenes involving cannibalism are guaranteed to gag a glutton.)

According to Vane (he created all the dialogue, remember), this
is how seasoned Indian-fighting soldiers conversed and com-
ported themselves:

Lieutenant Bernard: "Where are those Apaches heading, sir?"
    Major Pilcher: "Beats the shit outta me."

Major Pilcher: "Lemme tell you, Barrett—I've been in this country
so long that when I came here, Pike's Peak was just a hole in the
ground, but I never saw the likes of this. We're camping right here
till I figure it out. I'm not goin' back to Fort Huachuca without
Geronimo's scalp."
    Joshua Barrett (cynically): "Then, I suppose, you'll get promoted
to colonel?"
    Major Pilcher: "Unfortunately, that won't make much difference.
I've killed over one hundred braves since '69. I was a captain five,
long years. Been a major seven. I put my life on the line for seventeen hundred bucks a year. Piss most of it away on liquor, women,
and cards. Won't never be a colonel, friend—not long as I'm judged
by the back-slapping, ass-kissin' bunch from the Point."
    Barrett: "Can I quote you?"
    Major Pilcher: "Not on your life. I have one year to retire." He
thrust his hand with his middle finger extended toward the rim of
the canyon. "Then, up the generals' asses!"

Then we have Venable Brown, "smashed altogether" on an
Apache liquor called tiswin and "looking like a heap of sorry deso-
lation," reciting what he calls "the miner's Ten Commandments."
The recitation lasts for three pages; the sixth of the 10 is sufficient

to give you an idea of this particular hunk of lunacy.

"Neither shalt thou kill thy neighbor's body in a duel. Neither shalt thy destroy thyself by getting tight nor slewed nor high nor corned nor three sheets in the wind by drinking smoothly down brandy slings, gin cocktails, whiskey punches, rum toddies nor egg nogs. Neither shalt thou suck mint juleps nor sherry cobblers through a straw, nor gurgle from a bottle the raw nor take it neat from a decanter; for thou art burning the coat from off thy stomach. Thou wilt feel disgusted with thyself and inquire, 'Is thy servant a dog that he doeth these things?' Verily, I will say, farewell, old bottle, I will kiss thy gurgling lips no more. And thou, slings, cocktails, punches, cobblers, nog, toddies, and juleps, forever farewell. Thy headaches, tremblings, heart burnings, blue devils, and all the unholy evils that follow in thy tram...."

Here we have Venable and Old Gabe, in another drunken exchange:

"The only good Indian is a dead one, right, Gabe? Just what they always said about niggers."

"*And* Jews." Gabe straightened up. "I ought to know!"

Venable eyed him derisively. "You a Hebe?"

Gabe flared his chest proudly like a mating pheasant. "My momma was."

"Don't believe it." For the moment, Venable relaxed from his watch. The only Jews he had ever seen were tight-assed shopkeepers in the cities. Jews were about as welcome in the West as Apaches.

"No. Gabriel in the Bible was a Jew same as me. I play a Jew's harp, don't I? That's a dead giveaway."

"Prove it." Venable's face leaned closer to him. "Let's see your pecker."

"You'll have to kill me first!"

And finally—Norman Thaddeus's crowning achievement—here is Venable, drunk yet again (the survivors do a *lot* of drinking in the Caves), serenading Baby Doe Trabber with a frolicsome little ditty:

"One, two, three, four,
I don't care if I go crazy,

> Long as I can pull my daisy,
> I don't care if I die, die, die—
> Long as I can see it fly!"

Those gallant frontier folk sure knew how to laugh in the face of death and danger, didn't they?

"Nix on th' pisen, Abner! I'm trustin' yuh hombres same ways a white ca'f trusts a alligater, the which is onfrequent an' some diluted with reflec'shuns an' ponderin's on th' fra'lty o' inhuman an' animal natur'. Le's hit the grit, Jack, an' take a sniff o' the prairie ozone, the same bein' oncontomernat'd with th' breathin' o' snakes an' polecats."
—Christopher Culley, McCoy of the Ranges

They camped that night by a narrow stream, and lit a big fire to keep off prairie dogs and wolves.
—William K. Reilly (John Creasey), War on the Lazy-K

6. "High in the Noonday Sky, A Lonely Coyote Circled"

It may surprise some readers to learn that a segment of the British population (and a segment of the Australian population as well) are ardent fans of Western fiction. It isn't much of a phenomenon, however. A love of adventure is part of the English nature, as witness the history of the British Isles and its peoples' far-ranging exploration and colonialism. Given such a passion for the thrills and hazards of far-off places, it's only natural that some Brits would find the colorful, exciting history of the Old West, coupled with the larger-than-life heroes and villains of Western myth, both fascinating and appealing. Many Englishmen traveled to the American frontier in the 19th and 20th centuries, for visits, hunting expeditions, and other reasons; and a large number of these stayed to establish permanent residence. The same lure led armchair adventurers to experience the Wild West vicariously.

A second factor is the Western story's kinship with the Northern. Canada, after all, was once a British territory and is still a member of the British Commonwealth; citizens of the U.K. have a vested interest in how their Canadian cousins fared on the Far North frontier, past and present. Northern-adventure stories were enormously popular in Britain from the early 1900s until World War II, and although their popularity waned somewhat after the war, as it did in this country, this type of fiction is still well regarded among discerning readers.

Western films and radio and television programs were a third factor in establishing the genre in England. Films starring John Wayne, James Stewart, and Randolph Scott brought out long queues at neighborhood theatres. William Boyd's Hopalong Cassidy was a favorite on early British TV. And Roy Rogers, Gene Autry, Tex Ritter, and other singing cowboys toured the United Kingdom in the '40s and '50s with great success.

Most of the Western fiction available to British readers prior to 1930 was imported from the U.S. Pulp magazines such as Street & Smith's *Western Story* had U.K. editions, and nearly every major publishing house, from Hodder & Stoughton and Collins on down to the lending-library publishers such as Ward Lock and Wright & Brown, maintained lines of Western-novel reprints by American writers. But the demand grew so great, and the aggregate returns so attractive, that publishers began bringing out originals in increasing numbers. Many of these new works were likewise written by Americans, some of whom forged substantial careers by directing their yarns exclusively or predominately to the British marketplace. Charles H. Snow, a prolific talespinner who had limited success in the U.S., was one; others include Charles Wesley Sanders, Gladwell Richardson, and, later, Lauran Paine.

British fictioneers, of course, were eager for a scoop from the Western beanpot. Far and away the most successful were those who emigrated to the U.S., took up residence in the West, and developed or nurtured abiding interests in its history. Such writers as L. L. Foreman, Arthur Henry Gooden, and Fred East (who wrote as Tom West) produced stories and novels that had a more or less convincing ring of authenticity. In the case of Foreman, the best of the British expatriate Westerners, his work earns the highest compliment of being indistinguishable in terms of style, background, characterization, and quality from that of his better-than-average American peers.

Those British Western writers who had less talent and ambition and who stayed home had a much more difficult time of it. The first original American Western pulp appeared in the U.K. in 1935, and a few others followed; but payment for stories was rock bottom. And as Steve Holland writes in his 1993 history of U.K. paperback publishing, THE MUSHROOM JUNGLE, "It was almost impossible for [British authors] to sell to the American magazines, as one author found. '[The Americans] have an exclusive way of their own of doing them,' he told a fellow scribe. Hardly surprising, since the Western was exclusively an American genre of writing."

British book publishers offered a more receptive, if not particularly lucrative, outlet for homegrown horse opera. George Goodchild, who also wrote Northerns and a popular series of detective stories featuring Inspector McLean of Scotland Yard, was one of the more accomplished early purveyors. A generation later, Matt Chisholm (Peter Watts), Kingsley West, and J. T. Edson, among others, would generate readable and reasonably well-researched, if somewhat less than distinguished, Western novels.

An Australian, Leonard F. Meares, rivals Lauran Paine as the single most prolific author of Westerns. Under his primary pseudonym of Marshall Grover, Meares published the staggering total of 700-plus novels for the Australian and British markets over a period of less than three decades, some three dozen of which also saw print in the U.S. in the '60s and '70s under the name Marshall McCoy. (Paine, no slouch, has well over 500 book-length Westerns to his credit, plus another couple of hundred mysteries, romances, and nonfiction works.)

Still other U.K. oat-growers, a couple of whom enjoyed a certain vogue for a time, yielded crops of alternative abundance. These lads, through shoddy research, misconception, indifference, lack of ability, just plain folly, or a combination of foibles, never quite managed to properly simulate Old West locales or the people who inhabited them. The Western milieu they created is a curious and often hilarious one that exists in a series of fantasy universes, each one different from the other in sometimes subtle, sometimes radical ways.

One such individual was Christopher Culley, author of a score of novels and short-story collections in the '30s and early '40s featuring a tough Texas Ranger named Billy McCoy. Culley's yarns are full of slambang action, plenty of romance, and lavish descriptions of a Western landscape that existed nowhere except in his own imagination. But his most memorable alternative trait was the invention of some of the more ridiculous "Western" vernacular ever committed to paper. One example from his 1935 collection, MCCOY OF THE RANGES, heads this chapter. Here are a couple of others from the same volume:

> "Fella citizens," roared Jake. "I'm riz up here in this mermentus time o' crisis an' misfort'on to purtest agin the doin's o' all dawg-gorn sher'ffs an' sichlike interlopin' ballyhoos, as is riz up in our midst, a-buttin' in an' disturbin' o' th' public peace. An' I'm pur-posin' accordin', as how we-all hits it fur the jail an' turns loose this here 'Walleye' Johnson, an' invites him cordial to a free-fer-all jamboree at th' expense o' this yer commoonity."

> "By hell, Sam's gittin' mighty dam' careless, if he ain't packin' a gun't shoots both ends an' one side."
>
> "Comes o' waitin' thar, chewin' an' talkin'! Now that galoot's out I'll betcha. An' what'n hell are we goin' t'duh?"
>
> "Duh? Ride up an' ax. An' ef he ain't there, wait on him comin' in. An' I guess firs' thing we bes' put thet gardarm greaser kid wh'ar he won't tell no lies."

🐎 🐎 🐎 🐎

Then there was Oliver Strange. An editor for most of his adult life in the periodicals department of a large British publisher, Strange was fascinated by the American scene; but when he wrote his first horse opera, THE RANGE ROBBERS (1930), he had never visited the U.S. nor done any serious research into the history, lifestyles, or geography of the West. THE RANGE ROBBERS was intended as a one-shot lark, but it was met with such favor by readers that his publisher encouraged him to bring back the novel's protagonist, an outlaw gunfighter cum knight errant known as "Sudden," in a series of books. Ten such books followed, nearly all published between 1931 and 1942. Seven of the 11 total appeared in this country, under the imprints of such respected houses as Dial Press and

Doubleday. Proof positive that even the best editors have inexplicable lapses in judgment once in a while.

In an essay on Strange's work in the second edition of Twentieth Century Western Writers, Fred Nolan describes the Sudden stories as "muscular," as having "complex plots and tremendous verve and pace," and as being "furiously readable." Be this as it may, they also have, Nolan admits, "fairly predictable ingredients," villains who are "black-hearted wretches straight out of Victorian melodrama," and a manufactured lingo that is an "odd mixture of formal English and mythical vernacular."

Strange's lingo is even stranger than that. Every male character in his novels speaks a phonetically spelled patois composed of one part bastardized Western pulp of the Christopher Culley sort, one part Oliver Strange alternate-universe Old West, and one part pure cockney. As in these examples from Sudden Takes Charge (1940):

"What's the giddy game stickin' us up this-a-way?" he demanded.

"Helluva note, ringin' in a perishin' tramp."

"That'll teach these glory-huntin' sots not to come pirootin' around here like they owned the place."

"I'm a lone wolf from Pizen Springs an' I'm here to blow this prairie-dawg community to hellangone. Emerge from yore holes, you varmints, or I'll smoke yuh out."

"Most unsocial beggar I ever met up with," the deputy remarked.

"Remember, dyin' on a empty stomach is a mighty dangerous thing to do."

That perishin' beggar of an alternate universe Western cockney also rears his giddy haid in Strange's action scenes.

Sudden sprang in, his right [fist] drawn back for the blow which should end the battle; he had the fellow at his mercy and there was nothing of that in his hard face. The beast had maligned a good woman....

Sudden's right fist shot up from below and landed just over the heart. It was a fell stroke, one which might have killed a weaker man.

The badgered man's eyes bulged; in some mysterious manner one
of the beggar's guns had leapt from its holster and was pointed at
the pit of his stomach.

🐎 🐎 🐎 🐎

The post-war paperback boom in the U.S. was matched by a
similar one in England. Paperback originals were then not new in
the U.K., as Steve Holland points out in THE MUSHROOM JUNGLE;
they had been popular with readers of cheap genre fiction for
many years. But in the late '40s and early '50s, the number of titles
and quick-to-cash-in publishers mushroomed. Such houses as
Gramol Publications, Gerald Swan, Amalgamated Press, Modern
Fiction Ltd., Wells, Gardner, Curtis Warren, Scion, and Badger
Books flooded the newsstands with thin digest-size and standard
paperback originals of every type and hybrid of category fiction.

There were racy gangster and private-eye stories with lurid
hard-boiled titles: DAMES PLAY ROUGH, STIFFS DON'T SQUEAL, TAKE
IT AND LIKE IT, DEAD BONES TELL TALES, ANGELS BRUISE EASY, DUCH-
ESS OF DOPE, NO MORTGAGE ON A COFFIN, THE CORPSE WORE NY-
LONS, and LADY, THROW ME A CURVE. Ostensibly written by virile
types with such monikers as Spike Morelli, Darcy Glinto, "Griff,"
and Brett Vane, they were set in alternate-universe American locales such as "Cincinnati City." There were science-fiction and
horror yarns: MAMMALIA, CHLOROPLASM, THE WHISPERING GORILLA,
and (shades of a Saturday-afternoon cliffhanger serial) THE HU-
MAN BAT VS. THE ROBOT GANGSTER. There were love-and-lust heavy-
breathers: STREETS OF SHAME, FLAMES OF DESIRE, BIG TIME GIRL
SHE'S DYNAMITE. And of course there were Westerns.

The titles on the British paperback gunsmokers tended to be
more pulpy than lurid: BUZZARD BAIT, SIX-GUN SAGA, RANGE
WOLVES!, DINERO TRAIL, THUNDER GUNS. Each novel was short, no
more than 40,000 words, and published in 64-page, 96-page, or
128-page formats, depending on publisher, length, and size of type
(Amalgamated Press brought out its Western Library series in 64-
page, dime-novel-style booklets with eye-straining type set in
double columns). Each had standard pulp ingredients, with pref-
erence for ranch-and-range yarns about rustling and other nefari-

ous doings; main and secondary characters alike were stick-figure stereotypes. The emphasis was on action, with as much gun-thunder crammed into their brief story lines as could be managed.

"As Westerns were the 'easiest' type of fiction to write," Steve Holland notes, "they were subsequently rewarded at a lower rate of pay to the [other genres]." The average rate for originals was roughly $2.00 to $3.00 per thousand words. "One author received the princely sum of £10 [approximately $40–$50 at the exchange rates of the period] for his full-length novel, and that was not an isolated case." Such oaters, therefore, were generally penned by the worst of the Grub Street hacks, as their plots, prose, and "Western" milieus clearly indicate. The best of the mushroom Western originals are simply forgettable. Ah, but the worst of them...

A cattlemen versus sheepherders farrago entitled GUNS OF GILA VALLEY and written by somebody masquerading as Tex McLeod, for instance, which is distinguished by such cockamamie passages of dialogue as:

"On yore laigs, buzzard!" he threw out. "Bust the breeze outa hyar onless you crave lead-pizenin'!"

"Try f'r a break," came the harshly-worded warning, "an' I'll blarst yore inside tripes to hellangone!"

"Well, Sam, I'll be dod-blasted!" he creaked.

"You may of had the edge on me thisatime, damn you, pelican. But I ain't done with you yit—not by a lawng ways. Next time I lamp you, it'll be the six-gun showdown. *And I'll come a-smokin'!*"

"Git to perdition," slurred out Farnes. "Yore bushwackin' pardners ketched their needin's. And you'd land the same fate if I had my way...."

"Your fust mission [is] to ride undercover into Hellfire Valley and put the deadwood on the rotten scum what salivated Ken—Hog Wilder and his sheepherdin' gaggle. What you say?"
    "Keno," crisped Del and held out his hand.

Keno. Any genuine brushpopper who said that would have had

his backside hooted and booted clean off the range.

🐎 🐎 🐎 🐎

Then we have a range-war lead-spitter, Saddle 'n Ride, by
Webb Anders, which has a similar brand of colloquy, some of the
more cockeyed "Western" euphemisms, and the most unlikely
posted sign in all of oaterdom.

> "C'mon, spill ut, Nate. I'm honin' to get the lowdown on this play.
> Sounds kinda' interestin'."
>
> "Hold hard, durn it, they's no great rush," came back Boswell,
> tantalizingly taking his time in regaling his sidekicker with the tit-
> bit of news he had in his possession. "I'm comin' to it. The way it's
> gonna go is this, pal: Boothill has laid a big deadfall f'r thet pesky
> State lawdawg, Bud Austin, and the cowmen. An' it's one what
> cain't hardly fail nohow."
>
> "G'wan," muttered his friend. "I'm listenin'—with both lugs."
>
> Nate chuckled. "Yeah, it's a brass-riveted double cinch this time
> awright, Jem boy. Yuh see, them blarsted cow-nurses done fixed
> reg'lar range patrols. T'other night…Lanny Keithson ketched a plug
> in the belly and cashed in his chips. Now Boothill didn't fancy thet,
> he didn't fancy it at awl. So he fanned in directly to see the bawss.
> Nex' day, we shipped out a haff-gross cans of blarstin' powder to
> the hangout in the saloon waggin."
>
> Ferrers did not happen to notice the rough-looking man who was
> standing at the far end of the counter, staring hard at him. Neither
> did he notice that man as he hurried away to rap on a door marked
> "PRIVATE—KEEP OUT, YUH!"

🐎 🐎 🐎 🐎

And then we have Timber Line, which was written by one Oscar
Kennard, surely the crown prince of British Western hacks whoever he was, and which is distinguished by a little bit of everything
atrocious. Such as its hero, the tough and laconic Marden, whom
Kennard characterizes thusly:

> There was a streak in Marden's make-up that was always warning
> never to put one's whole trust in any one person, friend or foe.

He slept with only half his senses dozing.

Marden was alone on the shadowed veranda, alone with his thoughts and conscious of a strange unease to which he was not accustomed.

His heroine, Nina, "the little bandido brat," is described in even more pithy terms.

Ordinary girls in this part of the territory did not go around with a hogleg so slickly oiled and tailored that an iron would near enough jump right up to the hand in moments of need. Ordinary girls weren't familiar with details of gunfighting technique such as that.

When she looked up and across at Marden, [her] black eyes were gleaming excitedly, alight with the spark of emotion too turgid to remain concealed.

"The boy...belonged to a renegade bunch," she said in a low voice. "He heist me [sic] an' made a play at me. Durned near tore the clothes offen me back. Jest like any other woman would, I figured it was me he wanted. I was kinda resigned to the inevitable, y'see. An' then I fairly gaped when I saw it was me fancy gear he wanted, not me. Feller, that's a blow to any woman's pride!"

Here is the villain of the piece, Sancho Proverde, head of "a mob of outlaw greasers":

He...wore immaculate and richly embroidered velvet, white silk shirt, tight black pants held in place by a scarlet sash over which was the bulge of a pawky paunch.

Here are a couple of Sancho's henchmen:

The door...opened and a lean, raw-boned man with crowlike shoulders and a flat black hat appeared. His clothes, too, were all black, rusty black and with an unkempt appearance. The only touch of colour about him to relieve this sombre exterior was the soiled white shirt he wore.

Marden kicked the gun away out of reach, taking no chance. The man had died too swiftly for his liking, but when he rolled him over he found that he certainly was dead....

He was an unprepossessing character. Even in death it was easy to see the case-hardened marks of the killer in his face.

And here, finally, a few more passages of Kennard's glorious prose:

They fled, with Marden and Nina firing back over their horses' rumps at the closely-bunched group of riders coming up astern.

He turned away and continued on to the big dim livery barn, redolent of horse smells, gloom and coolth, the scent of hay and corn and the rustle of contented animals.

"Lissen, son, I don't mean you no hurt, mind, but if you *do* ketch up with a certain young filly who's on the prod around these parts jest watch y'r step. That dame is dynamite!"

"Is that so...?" drawled Marden slowly. "Howcome you know so much about it, feller? What's the lay?"

More bullets trundled across the room.

ᛘ ᛘ ᛘ ᛘ

Trundling right along, we come to my favorite concocter of alternative British Westerns—John Creasey.

Yes, the very same John Creasey who published the labor-intensive sum of 540 novels between 1932 and his death in 1973 (another score or so saw print posthumously), under a plethora of pseudonyms. As a crime-story writer—the bulk of his output was in the mystery and detective genre—he was both popular and, at least in his J. J. Marric series featuring London police commander George Gideon, critically acclaimed. One of the Marric novels, GIDEON'S FIRE, received a Mystery Writers of America Edgar for best novel of 1961.

Early in his career, Creasey produced strings of novels in other areas of popular fiction: juvenile sports, aviation, and mystery stories, adult romances, and—shamelessly enough—Westerns. Beginning in 1938 and spanning a period of some 15 years, he was responsible for 29 bang-bang tales of the Old West published under a trio of pen-names: Tex Riley, William K. Reilly, and Ken Ranger. Only one of these, significantly, saw print in this country; just as significantly, the publisher of that lone U.S. title, WAR ON

THE LAZY-K (1946), was Phoenix Press.

In a marathon speech in 1969 accepting another and even more prestigious award from the Mystery Writers of America, the Grand Master, Creasey alluded briefly and humorously to his Western writing. He knew next to nothing about the American West when he decided to enter the field, he said, and so read dozens of novels by unidentified "popular authors" of the '20s and '30s to familiarize himself with historical and geographical background and jargon. But when he sat down to write his first horse opera, his knowledge was still so skimpy he made an immediate and embarrassing mistake. The opening line of his maiden effort, he said, was "High in the noonday sky, a lonely coyote circled."

This little anecdote is probably apocryphal, designed to draw a large laugh from his audience (which it did). The line does not appear in either of the two Westerns he published in 1938, ONE-SHOT MARRIOTT as by Ken Ranger and TWO GUN GIRL as by Tex Riley, nor have diligent researchers been able to find it in any of his other shoot-'em-ups. It *is* possible that he wrote the line and his publishers, who knew more than he did, deleted it before publication. Judging from some of the other stupendous gaffes he perpetrated that *did* see print, he was supremely capable of a lonely circling coyote.

Plotting and pace were Creasey's literary long suit, in whichever type of fiction he was indulging in; his Westerns are no exception. Their story lines, while built on such standard pulp premises as range wars (a preferred choice of his, along with the cattlemen-versus-rustlers story), were rather more complex than those of his U.K. counterparts and made sense within the established framework; and naturally they were loaded with fast and furious action. This is how one of his publishers, Wright & Brown, describes Tex Riley's THE SHOOTIN' SHERIFF (1940) in its jacket blurb: "Cattle on the run, guns smoking hot, the fight between justice and outlawry reaching a tremendous climax. There is not a dull page in this rousing story of [Texas] border country feuds and hatreds—the atmosphere of the Wild West is vividly presented."

Well, yes and no. The fact is, no matter how many American

Westerns by "popular authors" that Creasey read, no matter how much other research he did (if any), his version of the Old West in general and "Texas" in particular amounts to yet another never-never land—a sort of skewed British Westworld, in fact. The "Texas" in which all of his Westerns are set bears about as much resemblance to the real Lone Star State as Dover does to Dallas. And the errors he made, the misconceptions he held concerning flora and fauna, lifestyles, attitudes, accoutrements, and lingo, are multifarious and often quite funny.

In GUNS ON THE RANGE (1942), a Tex Riley smokeroo, Creasey describes the "Texas" border country thusly:

> Three-four miles on the Three-X side of the Ria [sic] the grassland gave way to scrub, some purple patches of sage, in places juniper, dwarf oak, and occasionally wildly beautiful stretches of wistaria. Wild flowers grew in abundance, yet in places were cheek by jowl with cacti, sprung there no one knew how, but flourishing more than on the mesa beyond, or on the deserts further south. Sometimes the grotesque growths stood twenty feet from the ground, great spikes shot in freak directions.

> There was a hush about everything, even the birds were quiet. But a blue cardinal flashed across their eyes, emitting its lovely song, and then other birds took up the cry, as if they recognized these men as friends, and knew that there was no danger from them.

> The trees, some of them dwarf oak but in wide patches nothing but cedar and pine, the latter spiking like arrays of church spires toward the limitless blue heavens, drew much nearer.

Just how far off the mark are these descriptions? For an answer to that question, I sent them (and the Creasey quotes that follow) to noted Texas writer and Western historian Dale L. Walker. His response: "I take it by Ria he means Rio, as in Rio Grande, which doesn't have much sage growing near it. 'Wistaria' must be 'wisteria,' a climbing vine-type shrub that does not grow in the southwest [or] anywhere in 'wildly beautiful stretches.' The 'cacti' (a word those old gnarly stove-up Westerners used a lot) he describes as being 'twenty feet tall' with 'great spikes shot up in freak directions' sounds like saguaro cactus, which does not grow in

Texas. It is an Arizona cactus. I don't know about blue cardinals; thought they were red. Even Catholic cardinals wear red hats. So do the St. Louis Cardinals."

Creasey's knowledge of "Texas" cattle was on a par with his knowledge of flora and fauna, as witness this observation in William K. Reilly's SECRET OF THE RANGE:

> There were two worlds, side by side, one arid and barren in mid-summer supporting neither man nor beast, the other fertile, and dotted with two thousand head of J.K. beeves, mostly short-horns, but with some Frisians [sic] and Guernseys among them—the Kenworth family believed in experimenting.

They certainly must have. Friesians and Guernseys are dairy cattle!

Creasey seemed not to have much of a clue about horses, either —strangely enough, given the fact that the English have always prided themselves on their horsemanship.

> His gray, a rangy horse not long from mustang stage but clearly produced from a horse which had been well bred and then escaped to the wilds of Texas to interbreed with wild horses, hit the trail steadily, making far more speed than its slowish, raking strides seemed to suggest. (WAR ON THE LAZY-K)

> A lone rider, jogging easily along the trail, on a magnificent bay pinto not long from mustang stage. (Tex Riley, RANGE WAR)

Evidently he believed that "mustang" was a stage of growth somewhere between colt and full adulthood. He also seemed to think that "pinto" was a synonym for horse, such as bronc or pony. In RANGE WAR he refers to both "bay pintos" and "roan pintos," and further deposes: "A posse, Bill knew, travelled only as far as its slowest pinto would allow."

Guns likewise had him fuddled:

> Bullets spat out at him, missing him by inches. Black had pulled up his bronc savagely, seeing Jim at his mercy.
> And then Black's gun fell on an empty barrel! (WAR ON THE LAZY-K)

Two bullets roared, shattering the silence. (Tex Riley, GUNSMOKE RANGE)

So did cowboy customs:

After a long silence, Jim took his tobacco bag from his pocket and slowly began to roll the makings. (GUNS ON THE RANGE)

For the reader not familiar with the term "the makings" (which is usually written with the "g" dropped, as "the makin's"), it means the tobacco—Bull Durham, most often—and paper with which Westerners fashioned a cigarette. The weed Jim rolled must have been something to behold. Besides, Bull Durham sacks are danged hard to light.

Creasey on saloon girls:

He watched...the women, all painted bezoms, eyes glittering with drops, gowns tawdry and bedraggled at hems and shoulders, low-cut and revealing ample bosoms. (GUNS ON THE RANGE)

Dale Walker again: "'Bezom' I don't find in my biggest diction-ary. Did he mean bazooms? If so, wonder why they were 'painted.' Also wonder what kind of 'drops' made the bezoms' eyes glitter. Visine, maybe?"

Creasey on Indians:

The coppery face, the hooked nose with the skin stretched tightly across it, and the narrow, slanting eyes were those of an Indian; and a man who knew that country well would have seen the touch of the Kiawa [sic] about him. Kiawas were the most bloodthirsty and cruel of the tribes of Texas, men who were not men, who dealt in pain and hate and torture, and little else. (WAR ON THE LAZY-K)

"Kiawas" may have been deadly foes constantly on the warpath in the "Texas" border country, but Kiowas migrated from the northern plains only as far south into Texas as the Staked Plains; and while they were often allied with the Comanches (as at the Adobe Wells battle), they were never found on the warpath any-where near the Rio Grande and the Mexican border. Nor were the Kiowas particularly cruel or bloodthirsty.

The Caucasians who inhabit Creasey's "Texas," heroes and outlaws alike, are red-blooded and virile, to be sure. But to a man they speak a dialect which, in Dale Walker's words, "no Texan, or Westerner afflicted not with brain-steam disease, ever spoke."

> "Yuh'n others seem t' fergit things, Carradine. The Shereef've any County in the Yewnited States signs a declaration of loyalty to those States, an' the Federal Gov'ment. More, he agrees to make statement of any time, the conditions of his territory get outside've the law. More...the Federal Gov'ment can an' will relieve any Shereef knowingly disobeying the law of his badge an' status." (RANGE WAR)

> "I'm workin' fer Perkiss, an' I started at sun-up. Leastways, to-day's the first of June, I reckon, an' the docket 've hire says I start that day. (GUNSMOKE RANGE)

> "Say, yowse guy—where's O'Daly?" (GUNSMOKE RANGE)

> "It sounds mighty good, li'l man. Yuh'll grow up one've these days ef yuh keep gettin' idees thataway."
> "Now lissen! I'm tellin' yuh ther' was idees in this head've mine 'fore yuh were thought of, yuh big-headed *cayuse* yuh! Jumpin' snakes, ther's more idees in my li'l box than yuh c'd think in yers!"
> "Orl-right—let's hear *yuhr* idees, Mistah!"
> "Waal, I'm thinkin' thisaway...." (RANGE WAR)

> "Why, yuh goddamned townee! I seen better riders'n yuh in knickerbockers, an' as fer Shereefs—lissen. I won't hev yuh talkin' thataway——" (THE SHOOTIN' SHERIFF)

> "Ah, go douche yer head in a pail ev water!" (GUNSMOKE RANGE)

And last but not least, here is what Creasey considered hearty fare for cowboys riding herd and in the bunkhouse:

> Pommel-bags were re-packed with flapjacks and beans. (RANGE WAR)

> Charlie had prepared a [breakfast] tray on which were boiled eggs, hot scones, butter and coffee. (Tex Riley, RANGE JUSTICE)

Cow-nurses in "Texas" sure had it good, what with all those boiled eggs and hot scones dripping with melted butter. Except, that is, when the ranch cook turned mean and packed syrup into the "pommel-bags" along with the flapjacks and beans.

Feigning sleep, the leanness of Hugh's buttocks let the shock of the leather-springed coach jar his spine.
—Brad Ward, THE BARON OF BOOT HILL

Bill had his right hand in his pants pocket, and from that hidden position something poked outwards menacingly in the stranger's direction.
—Anson Piper, THE PAINTED GHOST

7. A Plethora of Flapdoodle

This chapter is devoted to bits and pieces of alternative flapdoodle—nuggets rather than bonanzas of yaller stuff. (Some might call them fool's gold, but you and I know different, don't we?) These nuggets have been painstakingly gathered here and there, round and about, hither and yon over a number of years, and each one—regardless of size, shape, or texture—glitters bright enough to be worthy of display in the Alternative Hall of Fame.

Let's begin at the beginning; that is, with

Narrative Hooks, First Sentences of a Novel Division

"By the gods," I said, "if that's all the so-an'-so's hired me for he can stick his badge up his adenoids!" (Nelson Nye, CARTRIDGE-CASE LAW)

The Kid came out of the rain and walked in on Death. It was as unexpected as having your hat slide down over your ears. (Abel Shott, THE BULLET BRAND)

The young pinch-faced hombre and the girl, bathed in the scintillating sunlight that touched the jeweled valleys of the sparkling basin beneath the frowning line of the distant hills beyond the rangeland, made an incongruous pair. (Will Garth, LAWLESS GUNS)

He came one morning when the sun was a molten mass of hell in a brassy sky, and it took only one look at him to name him Trouble —with a capital "T." (Brad Ward, THE SPELL OF THE DESERT)

Riding down from the mountain camp where he had left old Luke
Stone, Satan Brail's keen ears caught the rattle of downwind gunfire.... (Johnston McCulley, GOLD OF SMOKY MESA)

Narrative Hooks, Opening Paragraphs of a Novel Division

Sunset blazed above the Guadalupes like the spilled paint pots of a
drunken artist-god. Orange and gold and scarlet and damask was
the flaming background, with highlights of salmon and rose and
chrome. Patches of sky like rain-streaked steel showed here and
there, their ragged edges tinted faintly as with powdered verd.
Shafts of amber lanced to the zenith, paling and thinning until
they vanished in the higher blue.

It was a stormy sky. Fantastic cloud masses, pulsing and dripping with color, climbed higher and higher. They were like mighty
mountains buttressing the causeway of the stars each with its core
of ominous black and its wrappings of spectral fire.

Beneath these sky-flung spires of nebulous change, the Guadalupes stood ponderous and gigantic, bastioned by eternal granite.... (Jackson Cole, RIDERS OF THE RIMROCK TRAIL)

To put in bald words the record of even a simple event is no small
task. Words are a pigment too watery to blazon the rich reds of
man's courage and the shadow blues of his fears. Words walk too
slowly to match a bullet's speed and speak too softly to echo a roll
of thunder down a midnight canyon, a woman's cry from the bed
of birth or the pulse pound of the human heart with the lift of
death's dark muzzle.

Words are too neat and circumscribed. How can they recall a
puzzle pattern that sprawls half a continent and spans full thirty
years? Words are too ponderous. Can they split the atom where
bravery and cowardice merge? Have all man's words, through all
his centuries, been able to state the formula of his love? No, words
are too blind to see beyond the windows of the soul or too dumb
to tell what is found there.

This, then, is apology. Name it so.

But it is apology for means and method alone. The matter in

hand needs no excuses, no scrape of foot or overhumble hat. It is fumbling fingers that ask indulgence, hesitating above the threads of scattered lives and tangled happenings and uncertain which to choose. (Jack Byrne, GUNSWIFT)

Anatomical Oddities

She saw Matt's hand streak over his chest, and then he was falling...falling...and she stood with the bitter taste of her heart between her teeth. (W. Edmunds Claussen, REBELS ROUNDUP)

Her throat was lovely, a graceful column swelling up from the deep cleft between her breasts. (Brad Ward, THE BARON OF BOOT HILL)

The bouncer was watching him, black hair dripping and shivering in the morning chill. (A. A. Baker, A NOOSE FOR THE MARSHAL)

With the cattle would be close to thirty riders, most longhaired and unkept [sic]. All were fighting men, hired and paid according to the number of notches on their butts. (Tom Roan, RAWHIDERS)

He had learned to do without [women]...until Poppy Ames unleashed his libido and put it out front where he could really see it. (Lee Davis Willoughby, THE GUNFIGHTERS)

Wacky Word Choices

A buzz of talk strummed behind him when he went out. (James P. Olsen, THE CURSE OF THE KILLER)

"A fine homecoming, Rojo hoss," Cole muttered, spurring the cayuse into a foxtrot. (Walker A. Tompkins, THUNDERGUST TRAIL)

A second report crashed out.... Now Jim Brown's body was falling even as the single explosion leapfrogged echoingly over the countryside. (Jack Kane, BUZZARD BAIT)

Dexter's...fat wife was so scared she was blubbering. (Dean W. Ballenger, GUNSLINGER JUSTICE)

Slap! The Mexican's brown palm hit his gun butt, but before he could swivel the halfbreed holster up for a shot, Cole's Judge Colts recoiled against the crotch of his hands. (Walker A. Tompkins, THUNDERGUST TRAIL)

Little ridges of muscle ridged his jaw. (Brad Ward, THE SPELL OF THE DESERT)

Outside the shelter of the canyon there was a veritable inferno of icy wind and driving particles of hard snow. (Leslie Scott, BRANT OF TEXAS)

Sundance's black eyes jabbed up a twinkle. (Clem Colt, GUNSLICK MOUNTAIN)

Other guns began blasting, their muzzles slobbering brief blooms of orange light against opaque darkness. (Leslie Ernenwein, BULLET BREED)

Fractured Similes and Metaphors

Huck Brannon had a headache. A regular skookum he-wolf of a headache—the kind that hopped about inside the head, leaping from brain cell to brain cell on hobnailed boots, crashing against the ceiling of his skull with spiked mallets and kicking an occasional iron hoof at sensitive nerve-centers for good measure. (Bradford Scott, THE COWPUNCHER)

The muzzle of his Winchester seemed to flinch. A ripping gash of fire jerked like a hot ribbon into the room with an all-drowning crash. (Tom Roan, WHISPERING RANGE)

…He lit a fat torpedo cigar that stank uniquely like barbecued dog turds. (Wesley Ellis, LONE STAR AND THE PHANTOM GUNMAN)

The gunfire on Waco's main street erupted in a whirlwind of eager men, like a twister changing directions. (Jack Kane, BUZZARD BAIT)

"Let me out of here!" blubbered the man, wheeling like a fish out of water to his right. (Tom Roan, GUN LORD OF SILVER RIVER)

The roundhouse swing was perfectly timed, and exploded like a ton of dynamite on Kelton's jaw, with the force of a mallet on the head of a steer. (Joseph Reardon, THE CERRO LOBO)

The sun rose like a fire arrow leaving the bow. (Jack Kane, BUZZARD BAIT)

The moon had risen as they rode, stood up, a thin slice of glowing matter set in ebon metal, in the sky. (Brad Ward, THE SPELL OF THE DESERT)

Over the tallest crags seemed to writhe and hover a tremulous mist that from time to time refracted the bloody sunlight like a shifting cloud of diamond dust.... It was as if the dark Spirit of the Hills was glooming there above the lurid battlements of its grim castle of evil.

Between the town and the gloomy hills rolled the smiling rangeland, bathed in rose and amethyst and amber-tipped green, like a cheerful page of good deeds between two records of evil. (Jackson Cole, LONE-STAR LAW)

Bender's heart banged around like a chained canary. (Clem Colt, TOUGH COMPANY)

The black mouths of tunnels...were like blood-clotted wounds at the foot of the mountain. Shafts whose round mouths said a distressed "oh!" to the arching sky. (A. Leslie, "The Texas Ranger")

Strange Transformations of Nouns into Verbs

The sun mid-morninged. (Dean W. Ballenger, GUNSLINGER JUSTICE)

His voice was manly and it came out like he was a man you'd best not lock horns with unless you were eager for a boothillin'. (Dean W. Ballenger, GUNSLINGER JUSTICE)

Physical Improbabilities

Kinstrey's eyes cruised forward. If they were lucky they should be across the Divide in a few hours and by nightfall make Woodford's on the other side of the mountain. (Clark Brooker, FIGHT AT SUN MOUNTAIN)

For with abrupt speed and an amazing amount of vengeful determination, the angry giant swung a vicious, hard-handed fist at Richard Harding Davis' head, which was half-inclined in the act of picking up the walking stick. (Lee Davis Willoughby, THE ROUGH RIDERS)

He urged his animal into wakefulness, and the green carpet of the valley floor began to fly beneath its feet. (Joseph Reardon, THE CERRO LOBO)

"There's no mistake? You're certain?"

"I was there. I saw it only minutes after it happened." (Lee Davis Willoughby, THE ROUGH RIDERS)

Action Sequences

That's when he saw Odd Boy Marsh.

That's when he saw slavering, red-eyed guts-and-blood-and-splintered-bones-death coming at him like a runaway prairie schooner.

That's when he saw the neck and shoulders of a hippopotamus, riding along on the body of an elephant. He almost shed his skin.

His blood seemed to curdle and he was certain he'd gulped his tongue, as he stood up, and, because he didn't have a chance to run, squared off.

He was tight, like the strings of a maniac's fiddle, he was tight. He was scared. He pictured his arms and legs and head being yanked off, the rest of him scooped up and wadded into a dripping chunk like a snowball. (Glenn Low, VIRGIN BOUNTY)

Whiz! The blazing torch smashed Curt Thode's whirling head square in the eyes.

Spang! At point-blank range, Deo Daley's pipestone-butted Peacemaker roared out its song of death [and] a red fountain spurted from a great slot in the middle of one of Thode's black sideburns.

Bang! Another six-gun bullet punched a gushing crater in the center of Curt Thode's sloping, satanic brows.

Bam! And Daley's third cartridge swept the evil Fort Adios traitor to the floor, the leaden missile ripping his treacherous heart asunder.... (Walker A. Tompkins, THE SCOUT OF TERROR TRAIL)

Promotion of Racial Harmony in Western Literature Award

One who knows Mexican character thoroughly does not call all of them knaves nor yet all of the knaves cowards. (Anthony M. Rud, THE SENTENCE OF THE SIX GUN)

"No Kidding!" Award

Buck pulled off the [dead man's] mask. A homely, bewhiskered face, emotionless and gaunt, met his gaze. (Lee Floren, COTTON-WOOD PARDS)

The Battle of the Sexes; or, Courtship of the Tiny-Brained Folk

With a scowl Tubac...turned his mind to thoughts of Honey Hair, who certainly was something to think of. That is not to say that his thoughts were *serious*. He might be the boneheaded yap Jinx had called him, but his head wasn't solid ivory! None of your frills and furbelows for *him*—there was not going to be any gal's apron-strings hitched onto Tubac Jones, by grab! Not on your mortal tin-type.

But she was a danged nice critter just the same, and he guessed bee trees was plain gall beside her; however, he wasn't going to think of her seriously. Too many guys had got hooked in that fashion—and some of them right good poker players, too. Girls were all right if you just kept your head. Gallin' was like eating striped candy, Jones thought, only you could take a dose of salts if you got too much candy; whereas if you got too much girl— Well, anyway, she was as handsome as an ace-full on kings, and the prospect of taking her hossback riding some night was nothing to get the creeps up about. (Clem Colt, GUNS OF HORSE PRAIRIE)

"I hope I never have to eat a worse meal."

She beamed at the compliment. "I want every man who goes out of here to feel the same way." (Giles A. Lutz, MY BROTHER'S KEEPER)

Dialogue Award—Hero (to banker's secretary)

"That's quite all right, ma'am. You just trot on in an' tell that swivel-eyed Mormon pirate either he's comin' out here or else I'm comin' in, pronto. I ain't figurin' to be stood off no longer! You tell him, ma'am, if him an' me ain't passin' chin-gab inside o' five seconds, I'm goin' to pull this temple o' Mammon down an' spank him with the splinters!" (Clem Colt, GUNS OF HORSE PRAIRIE)

Dialogue Award—Heroine

"I'd best whomp up the rest a the grits, Ma," she said. "Pa and Ross and that looksome stranger is likely to be hungrier'n all getout when they get through skidooin' that Oslander trash." (Dean W. Ballenger, GUNSLINGER JUSTICE)

Dialogue Award—Exchange Between Hero and Villain

"You unnameable!" Duane clipped in that too-quiet metallic voice. "You're the damned ghoul that——"

   "You can't call me names!" Ike Kirsch bawled that all might hear. (James P. Olsen, THE CURSE OF THE KILLER)

Dialogue Award—Cowboy to His Horse

"I ask you confidentially, Sloppy," he said softly, "do you feel anything. I mean sorta like—uh—well, like you was setting on a keg of gunpowder and a lit fuse smoke-dripping sparks? Look at that jasper over by the post office. By the swing of them two guns, he ain't no Sunday school teacher, not yet an honest rancher. And without even knowing my name is Ladigan—a handsome man—he don't like me. Tch, tch." (James Shaffer, SLEUTHS OF THE SADDLE)

Dialogue Award—Buscadero

"An' now, *amigos*," announced Curt Thode, like a ringmaster about to introduce the main spectacle of the circus, "you're goin' to see this pretty gal here die like a real castle queen should die. In the old days, they used to behead queens. An' there's a beheadin' machine right here, gang—a genuine guillotine!..."

"This here's the cleverest torture machine in Picadero's bunch. Watch, you hombres, an' I'll show you how it works.

"These two chains run down here to this trigger board, which is just like the trigger of a big mouse trap. We'll bolt the girl to the floor, with her neck in this board. Her head will rest up on this trigger. So long as she can keep her head up off the floor, she's all right. But when she gets tired an' lets her head rest down—*powie!* No more head." (Walker A. Tompkins, THE SCOUT OF TERROR TRAIL)

Dialogue Award—Drunken Bully

"I'm the evillest hombre alive! Whoopee! I hate all sheriffs! Last sixteen sheriffs I met, yuh know what I done with 'em? I tied their ears tuhgether, behind their heads, like haywire. An' hung 'em around on trees, like Christmas decorations! I'll wallop Blue Steele so dead he'll git fly-blowed before he hits the ground....

"I'm the ol' sinner from Bitter Creek. I'm full o' bad intentions, an' wherever I cast my shadder, the grass withers up an' dies!

"I'm a he-barrel cactus, full o' stickers! I'm set tuh squirt 'em out in all directions, like a porkypine! Yes sir, I'm mighty bad medicine! I use bullets tuh sugar my cawfee! If I warn't so dry, I could spit out a grass fire!" (Tom Gunn, PAINTED POST RUSTLERS)

Dialogue Award—Exchange Between Sky-Pilot and Mrs. Sky-Pilot

"My god, I married an animal!" Ralph said, disgust in his voice. "Can't you see you're a minister's wife?"

"I'm beginning to see a lot of things, Ralph. One of which is I made a mistake...in marrying such a pompous wee-wee!" (William W. Johnstone, TRAIL OF THE MOUNTAIN MAN)

Dialogue Award—Mexican Male

"Muzzles for renegade dogs!" the little Mexican screeched glee-fully. "Come get thee lead muzzles, sons of thee coyotes!" (Ed Earl Repp, GUN HAWK)

Dialogue Award—Mexican Female

"Nize girls no dreenk in place like thees. What ees your name, nize boy?... You no like that I call you nize boy? But one is yong so lee-tle time—and old—so long! Ver' well, I will not do it again—beeg Americano mans!" (Arthur Henry Gooden, SMOKE TREE RANGE)

Dialogue Award—Indian (Navajo half-breed)

"My herald priest and my nephews and sons—they know these four hombre. Hoss-thief and renegade paleface. Don't like-im. They make-im bad bargain with me just now.... Hy-yu-skookum! Go fetch-im duffle bags with cans.... You take all thees cans. No got more. Very sorry. You good hombre and paleface squaw nice squaw. I like-im both very much. I give-im more if I had-im. But this three duffle bags is all canned muck-a-muck old Gila Joe have in xacalli." (Kim Knight, NIGHTHAWK'S GOLD)

Dialogue Award—Indian (unspecified tribe)

One of the chiefs grunted. "Yeah," he agreed. "But me, Big Chief Baloney. Hear lot of talk from white men, many, many times. All white man's talk baloney. Me, I not believe'm too much. Lot of ba-loney." (Lynn Westland, TRAIL TO MONTANA)

Dialogue Award—Scotsman (in reference to a skunk on the loose)

"Grup him, mon! Dinna stand sae gowkit! Grup him swithe an' fling him oot!...

"Dinna shoot him in here! Dinna shoot, ye latherin' penny wheep! Put him oot, ye clatty frampler!" (Clem Colt, GUNS OF HORSE PRAIRIE)

Dialogue Award—Black Character

"Lawsy me, folks, that's one bad voodoo there. Noah had best watch hisself careful. They's a bullet lookin' fer him, sho' nuff.... Ain't nothing in this world jist an accident, Mars' Insul. They is omens us cullud folk unnerstands. Once evil gits stahted, ain't no tellin' when it gwine stop." (Orlando Rigoni, CLOSE SHAVE AT POZO)

Dialogue Award—Chinese Restaurant Owner

"'ow do, please? Yo all 'ungry?" (Gene Tuttle, IMPOSTORS IN MES-QUITE)

Dialogue Award—Chinese Cook (whose name happens to be Charley Ching)

"No, no!" he protested frantically. "Me no sovvy. Me long time go to bed. Screams wakem up. Hear feetsteps upstairs, comee down velly, velly fast. Me pilem out of bed. Comee quick. Missy see me she stopee, faintee." (Cliff Austin, HORROR RANGE)

All-Time Alternative Dialogue Award—Stagecoach Driver

The driver's name is Cussemout Crandall and his salty expressions are like no other in Western fiction or on this earth, the sort of speech that might have resulted if Gabby Hayes had been taken over by a not-quite-fully-formed alien pod creature. All of these mind-bending exclamations are from Cussemout's one and only appearance, Anthony M. Rud's THE SENTENCE OF THE SIX GUN:

> "I'll blazin'-bang admit right off, stranger, that the Guzman Lake an' Casas Grandes gangs is stempestious, pizen mean, ef y'u tackle 'em all to once. Shore, they're the drainin's. Arizony an' New Mexico don't sewer out any worse blink-blank leetle devils, hoss-thieves, an' the like. Mebbe a fair sprinklin' of blisterous, bow-legged *cholo* killers, who done slung knives too whem-gubblin' sudden-like, or spigged a .44 into another fella's back. Not akshel hi-yu gunmen like Jack Hostetter, Louis Wreen, an' them. Nope. I got a notion about fellas y'u might call reg'lar, brimstone-seared, top-notch, A-1 killers —like Gila Joe, mebbe."

> "Goober-gibblin' gumbats!" he chuckled, advertising his comparative sobriety by the use of that favorite by-phrase.

> "What the hell y'u mean? It shore takes a begroggled, hoof-whifflin' he-man to frown thetaway at me!"

> "Most all hell-consecrated bad men hops the border at one time or 'nuther, with Henrys or Winchesters dustin' up the heels of their cayuses, but on'y the real bad ones come back! The rest is plumb

scairt. It don't mean nuthin' to go, but it takes sulphur-cured, whing-diddled guts to come back."

"He was hellious as all gitout, a reg'lar wasspoodle at fannin' a six-gun."

"I wasn't tryin' to sell y'u *that* hrruff-goobled, horny-tailed hunk o' horizon!" [i.e. a ranch]

Said Substitutes

"Yes," he hmmmed. (Kelly P. Gast, THE LAST STAGE FROM OPAL)

"Yes," slobbered Verne. (J. E. Grinstead, GUARDIANS OF THE RANGE)

"No!" he gluttered. (Jack Byrne, GUNSWIFT)

"Got *you* spotted," he apostrophized the hidden rifleman. (Leslie Scott, THE BRAZOS FIREBRAND)

"Robbery an' murder! Good Lord!" he gusted. (Tom Gunn, PAINTED POST GUNPLAY)

"No use huntin' fer him in the dark," Hi gloomed. (Allan Vaughan Elston, COME OUT AND FIGHT!)

"What do you mean?" he stiffened. (Brad Ward, THE BARON OF BOOT HILL)

"This is one hell of a pore idear!" he yawped. (Tom Gunn, PAINTED POST GUNPLAY)

"Yuh blame right!" chorused Pronto. (Tom Gunn, PAINTED POST GUNPLAY)

Missing Sibilants; or, "Snake? Hell, Pard, I Don't See No Dang Snake"

"Better be careful," someone hissed from the shadows. (Lynn Westland, KING OF THE RODEO)

"Open the door, Billy," Fuller hissed. (A. A. Baker, A NOOSE FOR THE MARSHAL)

"Ahuh," he hissed. (Brad Ward, THE SPELL OF THE DESERT)

"That's for callin' me a liar, an' it ain't nothin' to what yore about to git, hombre!" hissed the prowler in a voice like the breath of a viper. (Walker A. Tompkins, THE BORDER EAGLE)

And finally, the category known simply as

Huh?

Spitted undignifiedly across the jagged spear of a broken [cactus] trunk splintered by lightning, the rider glimpsed a shapeless lump in the distance. (Anthony M. Rud, THE SENTENCE OF THE SIX GUN)

"Iffen I was you," the foreman said, "I wouldn't go stickin' my chest out over hazin' a think like Chandler." (James P. Olsen, THE CURSE OF THE KILLER)

To seem right and good in the eyes of a man like T.R. was the zenith in hosannas. (Lee Davis Willoughby, THE ROUGH RIDERS)

As his physical condition improved, his thirst to square matters with Captain Lovell became a bile in his throat. (Jack Kane, BUZZARD BAIT)

"My ol' pistolian ain't rusty," Sample grunted. "An' don't you tell me to keep my nose out; remember, I got a whacky comin' to me." (James P. Olsen, THE CURSE OF THE KILLER)

"I never stole no horse!" Ross Dexter, who was seventeen and practically man-growed, blurted, his scare coming out the way he squeaked it. (Dean W. Ballenger, GUNSLINGER JUSTICE)

His wiry biceps [were] taut against the cowhide jacket as he dropped his elbows to hitch up his pants. (Jack Kane, BUZZARD BAIT)

Gun-fighting a woman with a two-dose squirt-load of lead was medicine Shryke had no stomach for swallowing. (James P. Olsen, POWDERSMOKE PADDY)

Like the mythical Kansas jayhawk, that bird which flew backwards

—it didn't care where it was going but it certainly wanted to know where it had been—Wesley David Cardigan awoke the next day in his room at The State House, deeply perplexed. (Lee Davis Willoughby, THE GUNFIGHTERS)

During the early days in the Southwest—when women could shoot as accurately as men—the most dangerous nonsense a man could commit was to have a sexual affair with two women—who knew each other.

But Cyrus Bonner did just that!

In addition to his woman-trouble, Bonner had to worry about the Apache Indians who plotted to grab his Laughing Gun.

The Apaches believed that his gun shot "magic bullets."

A newspaper-woman concocted a story about his gun when she saw it in action, and wrote in her column: "Cyrus Bonner's gun laughs at chance." The Westerners then began calling it the Laughing Gun—and the article nearly cost him his life.

—Interior blurb for THE FURIOUS PASSION OF THE LAUGHING GUN
by Lynton Wright Brent

8. Of Galloping Lust, Virgin Bounty, Laughing Guns, and Doogin-Pins

"Western fiction has traditionally been clean," C. L. Sonnichsen says in a chapter entitled "Sex on the Lone Prairie" in FROM HOP-ALONG TO HUD: THOUGHTS ON WESTERN FICTION (1978). "Where the coyotes howl and the wind blows free was never a place for promiscuous sex, kinky sex, or perversion.... It is only in recent times that it has been put into a book like chiles or oregano into a *sopa*, and with just about as much emotional involvement."

To be sure, as Sonnichsen notes, plenty of romance may be found in the pages of Western novels and magazines throughout the first half of this century. But with a few minor exceptions, stolen kisses was about as far as it went. In the '20s the king of the Western pulps, Street & Smith's *Western Story*, took pains to assure its readers that it was a moral publication: Its cover logo in those days included the advertisement cum disclaimer, "Big, Clean Stories of Outdoor Life." Even such pulps as *Ranch Romances* and *Romantic Range* sold pallid variations on frontier relationships; in their pages you can find a great deal of boy-chasing-girl and vice

versa, but once the catch is made the curtain invariably comes
down without so much as that old standby, the ellipsis, to suggest
consummation.

Intimations of sexual activity lurk in the pages of a few Westerns authored by major names during the century's early decades,
particularly the novels of B. M. (for Bertha Muzzy) Bower, creator
of Chip of the Flying U and reputedly an earthy soul herself. Har-
old Bell Wright's THE MINE WITH THE IRON DOOR (1925), Zane Grey's
THE VANISHING AMERICAN (1925), and Edgar Rice Burroughs' THE
WAR CHIEF (1927) each presents love matches between Indians and
whites, with sexuality hinted at in each case.

The one truly daring Western novel of the period is Homer
Croy's WEST OF THE WATER TOWER (1923), in which a small-town
Missouri couple engages in out-of-wedlock lovemaking that pro-
duces an illegitimate child. The book's publisher, Harper & Brothers, found it necessary to bring out the first edition anonymously,
ostensibly because Croy had theretofore written "light fiction" and
his new novel was a serious sociological study of small-town life;
readers and book reviewers, the Harper mavens told Croy, might
become confused or irritated and give WEST OF THE WATER TOWER
poor notices that would harm his career. The real reason for the
author anonymity, of course, was concern that Croy's reputation
would be harmed by the novel's sexual content.

But Harper's fears were groundless. WEST OF THE WATER TOWER
became both a critical success and a bestseller, film rights were
bought by Jesse Lasky at Paramount Pictures for a then record sum
of $7,500, and Croy—who had never made any secret of his
authorship—had the added satisfaction of seeing his publishers
relent and issue subsequent editions with his name boldly dis-
played.

In the '30s, shudder-pulp magazines such as *Horror Stories* and
Terror Tales—and some detective and adventure pulps as well—
began selling a relatively mild form of sadomasochistic sex to
readers. Their gaudy, full-color covers (and black-and-white interior illustrations) depicted women in various stages of undress,
usually undergoing some form of torture at the hands of slavering

fiends; and the stories themselves, which bore such titles as "Virgins of the Stone Death" and "The Pain Master's Bride," delivered more of the same, though the menaced virgins were almost always saved before they could be odiously deflowered and the fiends were made to pay in blood for their crimes. Despite the popularity of this type of magazine, the Western pulps—with one exception—remained aloof. Their covers portrayed, as always, galloping mustangs, cowboys brandishing sixguns, and similar action scenes.

The exception was *Spicy Western*, one of a group of "Spicy" titles published by a Delaware-based outfit that rather amusingly called itself Culture Publications, Inc. From late 1936 until 1942, when pressure brought by "public decency" bluenoses forced Culture Publications to change their group name to Speed (as in *Speed Western, Speed Detective*, etc.) and to tone down their contents, Spicy authors larded their stories with as much sexual innuendo, voyeurism, and heavy breathing as the law would allow.

Spicy Detective and *Spicy Mystery* were the "hottest" of the group's books; *Spicy Adventure* and *Spicy Western* were less explicit, perhaps on the theory that readers of adventure and Wild West stories were less horny than readers of blood-and-thunder mysteries. In any case, the euphemistic sex in *Spicy Western* was pretty much limited to lavish descriptions of "milky white thighs" and "creamy globes straining at their wispy restraints." Now and then, one of the authors would wax a bit more poetic on the subject of mammary glands—

> Her little breasts, pert, like young apples, were peeping forth from their flimsy bondage. Miles thought they were the most fragile fruit he'd ever seen. (Stuart Adams, "The Arizona Kid")

—but for the most part, the sexual detailing was a mix of the "Golly gee" blush and the "Hot damn" leer. A perfect example is the following excerpt from Francis Steele's "The Sonora Ghost Rides," in the magazine's premier issue; this is about as hot as things ever got in the pages of *Spicy Western*.

> "Your skin's like the white of the chalk cliffs on the Hopi mesa,

ma'am," he said. "I bet it's soft an' warm like, such as them cushions over yonder on the bunk. I mean, ma'am, if a man could kinda touch it."

She came closer. The fragrance of her was heady, like pampas grass when it's tender.... Her fingers worked a button loose, another and another. Her dress sagged in front, showing the upper slopes of her satin smooth round breasts reaching out, warm globes of promise that vibrated with her every breath.

The Sonora Ghost's arms were like any other man's. He put them around her and jerked her to him. Her pliant body molded to his, her soft breasts throbbing against his chest, and when his hand brushed down her back, to urge her closer still, her body strained to him. Her breath, warm like her flesh through the thin material of her dress, bathed his face. She caught at his hand as if to guide it.

He held her off, suddenly. "You're no wanton, ma'am," he said fiercely through the hot rioting of his blood. "I'm thinkin' you ain't knowin' what you're doin' or you ain't sure-enough meanin'."

"I'm meanin'," she whispered.

As society became more permissive in the years following World War II, writers, editors, and publishers were quick to capitalize. Elliot Arnold's 1947 novel, BLOOD BROTHER, contains a fairly explicit (for its time) sexual relationship between an Arizona rancher and a beautiful Apache woman. A 1950 horse opera by Nelson Nye, RIDERS BY NIGHT, was the first traditional Western to feature an actual (and realistic) seduction. In 1953 the digest-size magazine *Gunsmoke*, published by the same company that produced the hard-boiled crime monthly, *Manhunt*, printed several stories with strong sexual overtones, among them Evan Hunter's tale of a brutal rape and its aftermath, "The Killing at Triple Tree." Western-magazine readers still weren't quite ready for such graphic goings-on, however; *Gunsmoke* lasted just two issues.

It wasn't until the '60s, when verbal and visual taboos started to unilaterally collapse, that explicit sex began to appear in Western fiction—mainly, at first, in contemporary tales such as Larry McMurtry's THE LAST PICTURE SHOW (1966). "Earlier novelists took us to the bedroom door," C. L. Sonnichsen laments. "Their successors...removed the door, and sometimes they walk right through the bedroom into the barn."

The first alternative horse opera in which the door was re-moved is Glenn Low's VIRGIN BOUNTY—something of a trailblazer in the soft-core-porn industry, in fact, given that it was published in 1959. Its publisher was Camerarts, a Chicago outfit that special-ized in "big, exciting manly shockers." Their Merit Books and Novel Library lines, which flourished from late 1958 until 1963, for the most part offered hard-boiled crime stories in the Mickey Spillane knock-off mode, with such inspired tittles as DAMMIT, DON'T TOUCH MY BROAD!, UNBELIEVABLE 3 & 1 ORGY, TORTURE LOVE-CAGE, SEDUCTION ON THE RUN, and BRUTE MADNESS.

Now and then they would try something different as a test case. VIRGIN BOUNTY, a Novel Book, was their first Western—and the first paperback original ever to be cover-labeled "An ADULT West-ern." Their second oater, Oren Arnold's SIN TRAIL, appeared as a Merit Book in 1960. Neither was successful, leading Camerarts thereafter to confine its lust-and-sleaze formula to contemporary themes.

Glenn Low, a former contributor to such pulps as *Ten Detective Aces* in the late '40s, was one of Camerarts' stable of prolific and manly hacks. Apparently on the basis of a couple of pulp-Western stories, he was assigned to write the company's first gunsmoker. Low, however, knew less about the Old West than even John Creasey and the British mushroom-jungle scribblers; VIRGIN BOUNTY fairly creaks from its overload of inaccuracies and anach-ronisms. Its plot, too, what there is of it, also creaks—the overload in this case being clichés. Its sexual content, and Low's sometimes eye-poppingly awful prose, is what makes it fodder for the alter-native bounty hunter.

The hero is an actual (well, putative) bounty hunter named Rand McKeever, "more man than Earp and Masterson put to-gether, and, when prodded, more animal than man." Unlike most Western heroes, McKeever has a weakness: Inside he is a mass of "hot, knotting sensations," the result of an extremely potent viril-ity. "Here lay his strength and his weakness. Here was what he had all his life feared would be his ruin. Not drink, not gambling, not

anything but women, beautiful, alluring women. And because of
his strength and this weakness, he had shunned them, chosen the
life of the manhunter."

As the story opens, McKeever is on the trail of a mortal enemy,
outlaw and gunfighter Trey Boland, and determined to keep his
libido in check at least until he captures Boland and delivers him
to the marshal in Apache City. But as the front-cover blurb makes
plain, "The odds—three hired killers, a sadistic sex maniac, and a
pair of greed-ridden prostitutes—were heavy against Rand Mc-
Keever. But the stakes were even bigger. Reward. Revenge. And 118
pounds of pulsating, naked Virgin Bounty!"

The first threat to McKeever's anti-nooky vow is the sadistic sex
maniac, who happens to be female: Josie Jewel, a.k.a. the Masked
Madam, proprietress of a sporting house full of hookers known as
Living Dolls. The mask she wears is a sort of snake-skin hood, and
nobody knows what she looks like under it. She, too, seems to be a
sexual abstainer, for obscure reasons; in fact, as she tells McKeever
when he encounters her on the trail, "I didn't agree to make the
trip [as a kind of chaperone to two of her Living Dolls who have
hired out to service Trey Boland and his gang] until he promised
that nobody would try to lay me. He swore he'd shoot the doogin-
pin off any man who so much as pinched my tit or smacked my
fanny."

One thing McKeever doesn't have to wonder about is Josie
Jewel's body. She soon reveals it to him, apparently by accident:
"Her green cloak parted. Her breasts, large and firm, plumped
through, small rosebud points thrusting vigorously upward from
halos of velvety pink." One glimpse is enough to start the hot,
knotting sensations somewhere in the vicinity of our hero's
doogin-pin, and to send him into rapturous (and anachronistic)
speculation:

> Wow! What a figure! What bubbies! What hips! Is she putting out?
> How much does she get? I'll bet it's plenty. She doesn't put out?...
> She's married, huh? No?... Is that so?... What's the matter with girls
> like that? They must want to. Cold-natured? Frigidity?...
> Hummmmm...Is that what it's called?

Despite all of this, McKeever really doesn't want much to do with the Masked Madam, since she's "as ornery as cat manure." His sensations are much more hot-knotted when he meets up with the 118 pounds of pulsating Virgin Bounty: Susie Cartwright (no relation to Ben and the boys on the Ponderosa), "a sweet little chump of a farmer gal" just arrived in Arizona from back east. Her bubbies are much more tempting, especially when it becomes evident that she is anything but cold natured and has no objections to the right man pinching her tit or smacking her fanny. And McKeever is the right man at the right time with the right dooginpin.

The consummation of their mutual lust, which comes about after a great deal of bloodshed and confused chasing around, is described thusly:

> She was pulling him through the darkness...walking backwards and hastily undoing his clothes. He began to tremble. He began to help her with his levis. His hands raced over her, eagerly, as though they had minds and intentions of their own. Her flesh felt cool and hot and soft and hard....
>
> She let go his levis. They fell to the floor. He stepped out of them. She was guiding him, her hands on his neck, his arms, his hips. She sat down on the edge of the bunk, lay back. He lifted her legs over the bunkside.
>
> He was over her on the bunk. She was moaning, murmuring, "I want to live I want to live I want to live I want to live I want to..."
>
> He looked into her eyes and breathed deeply.

Pretty hot stuff. But no hotter than the passionate sex scenes concocted by an alternative phenomenon named Lynton Wright Brent in a mid-'60s series of soft-core-porn Westerns.

Brent was something of a weedy Renaissance man. In addition to writing reams of marvelously terrible popular fiction, he toiled as a rancher, amateur historian, and B-movie actor. Acting was his primary avocation; he was an extra and bit player in silent films in the '20s, and in programmer talkies and the grand old Republic cliffhanger serials from the '30s well into the '50s. He had fifth billing (portraying a character named Matthews) in the 12-episode

Ken Maynard serial, *Mystery Mountain*, in 1934, and a somewhat lesser role in one of the better '40s serials, *The Adventures of Red Ryder*, starring Don "Red" Barry and Noah Beery, Sr. You can also catch Brent in the Roy Rogers flick, *Red River Valley* (1941), and in the Gene Autry saga, *Beyond the Purple Hills* (1950), among others.

As a writer of fiction, Brent was a whale of an actor. His first novel, THE BIRD CAGE (1945), is so bad he had to pay a vanity publisher to see it in print; this amazing "historical" Western will be accorded its just due in the next chapter. THE BIRD CAGE was his only novel from 1945 to 1964, when either he embarked on an orgy of creativity and produced more than a score of paperback originals over a seven-year period or, more likely, he dredged up and minimally rewrote material that had gathered rejection slips in years past.

In any case, in 1964–65 he published a dozen soft-core-porn Western, crime, fantasy, and love novels under the auspices of the Brentwood Publishing Co. of Hollywood; Brentwood's name and the fact that it published Lynton Wright Brent novels exclusively during its brief existence leads the trained deductive mind to presume that, with his own money or some poor entrepreneur's, he had founded his very own vanity publishing company. Masterpieces of the absurd, all, these books carried such inspired titles as LAVENDER LOVE RUMBLE, LESBIAN GANG, THE SEX DEMON OF JANGAL, THE FURIOUS PASSION OF THE LAUGHING GUN, PASSIONATE PERIL AT FORT TOMAHAWK, and LUST GALLOPS INTO THE DESERT.

The last three are Westerns, all of which have plots that might have been culled wholly from the worst of the Rogers and Autry films of the '40s. They also have numerous sex scenes that more than likely were grafted onto what were originally written as "straight" Western stories. No one could depict the sex act in quite the same nuttily eloquent fashion as Brent. Unfortunately, he had something of a single-track mind and a rather conventional imagination, and probably a lazy streak in his nature as well. All of his sex scenes have similar phrasing, similar grunting-and-groaning dialogue, and similar missionary positioning ("a man's rightful position is on top").

Let's start with PASSIONATE PERIL AT FORT TOMAHAWK, in which Army scout Gary Trader gets it on with Teen-na-ta, a shapely Pawnee whose voice "seemed to carry a soft glow and the scent of honeysuckle." But it isn't Teen-na-ta's voice that interests Gary. "His blood rushed madly through his veins as he feasted his glance upon her delicious curves and the fawn-like movement of her body. A thought ran wildly through his brain: *It's just a short distance up that skirt—to passionate love!*"

It isn't long before Gray has traveled that short distance—

With his free hand, he yanked the buckskin skirt high on her thighs. He glanced at the shapely legs done in brownish-velvet and grew highly excited. Quickly he fumbled with himself, and then made his plunge. The girl whimpered in muffled joy; and Trader struck his pace ruggedly and evenly. Her head was tossing madly from right to left, and her shapely lips were parted in an expression of delighted agony.

"Give it to me, Gary-love," she purred, "the staff of life and loving—"

Compare this to what happens in LUST GALLOPS INTO THE DESERT, in which Laredo Grant, unjustly branded an outlaw in the mining camp of Tombstone, gets it on with a shapely Indian wench under a sycamore tree. *He* gets excited when she "slipped her sweet tongue between his teeth and wriggled it frantically, sending lust charging through his veins." Then—

He slammed his mouth hard against hers. He struck a rhythmic pace, and was delighted when she responded readily. He felt her squirming with her urgent desire; and he drove harder, as though anxious to please.

She began kissing him like the rapid fire of a machine-gun. A glance down at the shapely legs clad in brownish velvet excited him mightily. The girl was whimpering in muffled joy; and Laredo struck his pace more vigorously. Presently the girl commenced tossing her head madly from right to left, and her shapely lips were opening and closing with her passion, like a fish out of water gasping for breath....

Laredo felt the explosion of her passion at the same moment that he was experiencing the same—and he kissed harder than ever before. "Holy cow!" he gasped, unable to restrain the extent of his pleasure.

The best/worst sexy Western by Brent is THE FURIOUS PASSION OF THE LAUGHING GUN, whose plot outline—no doubt written by Brent himself—is quoted at the beginning of this chapter. Cyrus Bonner's Laughing Gun is, of course, his Colt pistolian, which he uses to blow away numerous Apaches and a couple of gun-galoots, thus overcoming "FEAR, the Creator's caution-light." But his Colt isn't the only gun that gets a heavy-duty workout in this saga of lust and redemption. Janis Janet, the newspaperwoman who wrote the story about his Raucous Rod when she first saw it in action, could have written another one just as apropos after she "rammed her tongue into his mouth and gave his tongue the full treatment" during a moment of furious passion.

But she's fated never to wed Cyrus or his Hilarious Hogleg, as she realizes with "a tear sliding down her newspaper-calloused cheek." His true love is reserved for the beautiful and virginal (for one chapter) Avon Morgan, whose "shapely upper lip made him think of a day-old butterfly spreading its wings for the first time." He knows she's the only one when they get it on on the tailgate of her father's Conestoga wagon and "the thought struck him that no longer was she a virgin—and he alone was responsible for that!"

He kept working—steadily, solidly, vigorously.

"Give it to me, my precious darling," she whispered hoarsely. "I want more of your love staff."

She raised her hands and began playing them gently along the back of his shirt; and this action gave Bonner pimples he had never known before....

He was thrilled by the looseness, and the wetness, of her lovely lips as she applied them to his mouth and then his neck. When he touched her now with his fingers, around the face, he felt her trembling beneath him. He felt the great quiver which shook her body; and he groaned out to announce another peak-time.

Suddenly he heard voices. "Somebody's coming," he said.

As relatively explicit as the sex was in Lynton Wright Brent's novels, and in those of his paperback brethren in the '60s and early '70s, it was tame compared to that which began inflaming the pages of the so-called Adult Westerns in the late '70s. You couldn't get much more graphic than Jake Logan (David King) did in his Slocum series for Playboy Press, and its mix of no-holds-barred sex and violence resulted in huge sales and a glut of imitations and offshoots. This combination, as Western novelist and authority Loren D. Estleman wrote in a 1983 article for the WWA *Roundup*, "because of its built-in sensationalism and controversy has done more to rescue Western fiction from critical and popular dormancy than any number of artistic attempts to transcend genre." Unfortunately, as he goes on to say—

> With few departures…this subgenre bristles with anachronisms— not the least of which is the projection of today's moral values on the Victorian West—and the hero's adventures with cardboard baddies and the ubiquitous Colt are little more than an excuse to allow him to recover between bouts in bed. Its enormous readership, so out of proportion with the rest of Western fiction, suggests that the average fan of this new and inevitable form skips over the horses and gunplay, skimming the pages for a mention of feminine undergarments. The dedicated Western reader needn't fear that this pornographic prairie will swallow the frontier staple, because few dedicated Western fans have set foot in it.

Despite Estleman's positive prediction, the Adult Western's pornographic prairie very nearly did swallow the frontier staple. Throughout the '80s, in fact, it had the staple so far down its generally sleazy throat that the traditional Western was little more than an invisible lump—like a gopher being gobbled by a sidewinder. More than half of all paperback Westerns published during that period carried the "adult" label (and most of the ones that didn't were the product of a lone hand, Louis L'Amour).

Some series were remarkably successful; the Jake Logan Slocum novels, now being written by a crew of stablehands and published by a different house, have reached the age of legal consent and may soon reach the age of legal majority, with nearly 300 titles out so far. Tabor Evans' Longarm and J. R. Roberts' Gunsmith are also still alive and humping, though their age is showing after a couple of hundred titles each, and the last sunset (and last lay) for each draws nigh. (Gunsmith, it should be pointed out, is easily the best of the shoot-and-screw Westerns, with its creator, the amazingly fecund Robert J. Randisi, himself having penned more than 150 titles while maintaining an equally amazing level of energy and readability throughout.) Wesley Ellis' Lone Star was another long-lived series, lasting through some 140 titles before finally going limp, as it were, and biting the dust in 1994.

Some series came and went: Buck Gentry's The Scout, Patrick Lee's Six-Gun Samurai (featuring a Samurai warrior transplanted "from the land of the Shogun" to the American frontier), J. R. Longley's Angel Eyes (another series authored by Bob Randisi), Tom Cutter's Tracker, and Lou Cameron's Stringer.

One projected series failed to thrust beyond its premier volume: Jeff Wallmann's Bronc, "a lean, chiseled and gunslick bounty hunter" who also happens to be butt-ugly and pint-sized in every way except the one that counts most in an adult Western. Bronc's only adventure, BRAND OF THE DAMNED (1981), is a stewpot filled with all manner of alternative delights that its author swears were intentionally created as a kind of private spoof of the subgenre. Knowing Jeff as I do, after having collaborated with him on such howlers as "The Raid at Three Rapids," I'm inclined to give him the benefit of the doubt.

In any event, just a few of BRAND OF THE DAMNED's ingredients: a gang leader called Bobtail Kessler, a couple of buxom and super-horny wenches dubbed Prudence (a.k.a. Miss Pru) and Jasmine, a Sheriff named Winkle who is fond of calling Bronc "smartass" and "the l'il fart," cowhands with such monikers as Muttonballs and Fast-Mail Griswold, some wonderful pseudo-Western vernacular ("You ride with us, amigo, and you're riding with the top go-getters"), enough anachronisms to stuff a saddlebag, plenty of gunplay, plenty of hot sex, and such distinguished passages of dialogue as:

"You guys are all the same. All you ever care about is getting a girl in the sack."

"What's Harry doing out there? And why are his pants at half-mast?"

"I have to piddle."

"I like Miss Pru; I'd treat her like she deserves. She's a tolerable romp, and I'd cure her of bangtailing around."

"So you're wearing a nightgown. I don't care if you're starkers. I'm here on business."

"It's okay if you want me. After all, I'm a woman and you're a man...."

"If I'm getting too loose for you, I can put my legs together. That'll pinch me up tighter."

"You like your boobs sucked, don't you?"

✦ ✦ ✦ ✦

Of all the long-running adult series, the one most likely to provide chuckles is Wesley Ellis' Lone Star. For some reason its stable of wordsmiths seem to have been less serious-minded than those who regularly produced Longarm and others, and therefore more inclined to take a satirical approach to both plot and sexual content. One reason for this may be that "The Lone Star Legend" did not feature a brawny, lusty WASP male lawman or drifter or bounty hunter, as did most of the other shoot-and-screws; rather, its protagonists were "a magnificent woman of the West, fighting for justice on America's frontier," one Jessica Starbuck, and Ki, "the martial arts master sworn to protect her and the code she lived by." The idea of a beautiful, nymphomaniacal, justice-seeking gun-babe and a handsome, satyriasis-plagued half-Japanese and half-Caucasian companion trained as a Samurai warrior wandering around the Old West tilting at windmills and humping everybody in sight is so ludicrous that even the most humorless of the series' writers must have had a difficult time keeping matters wholly serious.

Some Lone Star novels reach extremes as ludicrous as the series' premise, tossing Jessie and Ki into such pickles as the one involving a mad scientist who is using cowboy slaves (some of whom glow in the dark) to mine pitchblende in Idaho, so he can experiment with virilium (radium) in a laboratory straight out of the original Frankenstein movie (#9: LONE STAR AND THE HARDROCK PAYOFF); and another whose elements include a mysterious and murderous rogue cougar (who turns out to be a man slicing up his enemies with fake cougar claws), a ruined hacienda packed with secret passages, and a group of Aztec priests who worship a jewel-encrusted idol to whom they sacrifice virgins in an underground lair (#123: LONE STAR AND THE AZTEC TREASURE). The sex, too, in some Lone Stars suggests that the author might have been cackling evilly when he wrote such passages as:

> Errol lunged up over her, and her hands clutched at his hardness, guiding it eagerly to the entrance of her empassioned hollow. His thick goad stabbed into her. Jessie twitched, feeling impaled, an agony of pleasure that grew sharper and tighter the deeper he skewered into her. She could feel his pulse from it. Errol breathed through his mouth, hugging her, forcing his girth into her hot depths, her insides igniting as he buried all of his huge invader. (#63: LONE STAR AND THE PHANTOM GUNMAN)

Another thing that turned a few veteran writers of adult Westerns into satirists, intentional or otherwise, was the strain of having to devise sex scenes with some measure of difference from one another. Loren Estleman again in his *Roundup* article: "The trouble with graphic sex in any kind of writing is that, literarily speaking, one act is pretty much like all the others, and the writer can describe various parts of the anatomy and their various functions only so many ways without becoming redundant."

Right. So what was the poor Lone Star or Longarm writer to do for the sake of variety in a single novel requiring up to six separate acts of copulation, and then again in the next book and in the one after that? Why, alter the *place* of each copulation, of course. That way, the same old clinical descriptions take on the illusion of freshness. Hence, the characters in adult Westerns not only get it on inside buildings, on beds, bunks, cots, couches, chairs, and floors; they also do it in the great outdoors on grass, sand, dirt, rocks, and moving conveyances such as trains, stagecoaches, buckboards, and buggies; and on horses running or standing still; and in lakes and mountain streams; and on fishing boats, riverboats, keelboats, canoes, and rafts; and in caves and those good old subterranean grottos; and in thickets and thistle patches, under waterfalls, in Indian teepees, on rooftops, and in cemeteries. In short, just about anywhere the human mind can conceive of two people (and sometimes more than two) satisfying the biological urge.

And that includes one additional location so audacious that only a skewed mind—or a brilliant satirist—could have envisioned it. In either case, it's the essence of alternative genius.

In a 1984 novel, TRACKER #5: THE OKLAHOMA SCORE, by Tom Cutter (a house name, naturally), the lawman hero and a buxom female companion are captured by outlaws and tied to the cowcatcher of a locomotive; and while the train is rushing headlong toward what seems to be their eventual doom, they decide they might as well have one last fling and so manage to work loose of their bonds just enough so that...

Yes! On the cowcatcher of a speeding locomotive!

"The Perils of Pauline," updated and X-rated.

O tempora! O mores!

Or to put it another way, in the words of a grizzled old sheriff in LONE STAR AND THE PHANTOM GUNMAN: "Sheer flamboozlin' horseshit."

He lifted his arms, stretching his long, lithe body in the sheer joy of being alive in the open, and dropped them to take a puff on his cigarette, regretfully watching its being consumed in that air it apparently drew in, too, with such gratitude that the tobacco was disappearing into blue curls of smoke far faster than he could have wished.   —Jackson Cole, THE OUTLAWS OF CAJA BASIN

Staring at the colored pictures, the sinews of Matt's body tingled. "She's beautiful!" he gasped inwardly.
Suddenly the flare in his own eyes fanned into a miniature inferno as, for a long moment, he was lost in despair. Of the countless times the single tragedy of his life had persecuted his reminiscence, not in many years had its recollection loomed so distressingly vivid as during this moment.   —Lynton Wright Brent, THE BIRD CAGE

9. Claws! Meets the Incredible
Shrinking Buckaroo

As we've seen in previous chapters, there are many different varieties of alternative-classic Westerns. It may be the peculiarities of one's plot that elevates it to its lofty status. It may be the unique mix of he-coons and she-stuff that inhabits its fictional terrain, or the nature of the fictional terrain itself. It may be the author's prose: his inspired use of Western vernacular, the manner in which he slings similes and metaphors, the brand of red-hot palaver he dishes out. Or it may be a combination of these and other, less clear-cut elements (genius, after all, is not always easily defined). The important thing is that in each work there is a savory blending of ingredients resulting in a peerless taste treat, a kind of fictional slumgullion stew for the jaded palate.

In this chapter we'll sample a few more potsful of perfection, two of which—the first and the last considered—your old prospectin' pard ranks in the Top Ten Pisswillie Whizzers of All Time.

BLACK GOLD, Jackson Cole

There are Western novels, and there are alternative-classic Western novels. And then there is BLACK GOLD, which is truly and quite literally in a class by itself. If I were to teach a course in the Alternative Western Novel, this is the book I would use as the centerpiece. It not only has everything a bad Western can possibly have, it brilliantly manages to go one step further: It has something no other horse opera has, a plot element so bold, so dazzling, so innovative, so casually insane that it left me awestruck when I first encountered it.

I wish I could tell you positively who deserves the credit for this masterwork, but I can't. Fact is, I'm not 100 percent positive which Jackson Cole wrote it. Judging from the prose style and other internal indicators, I *think* Leslie Scott; but since it is a Jim Hatfield yarn that first appeared in *Texas Rangers* in 1933 or 1934 (the book version was published in '34), and since Scott shared the Hatfield corral with Oscar Schisgall—and no doubt one or two others—in those days, and since there seems to be some bibliographic disagreement as to who wrote what Hatfield prior to 1937, we may never know for sure who was responsible for BLACK GOLD. More's the pity.

The basic premise is typical of the Jim Hatfield stories and barely intimates the wonders to come. As the William Caslon dustjacket blurb has it: "Into the big valley known as the Alamita Basin rode Jim Hatfield, faced with as tough a job of cleaning up a gang of organized exploiters as ever confronted the Texas Rangers. To this valley which knew no justice, which flamed with wild greed and unrest, where no one was safe from violent death, Jim Hatfield, the Lone Wolf, was to bring the RANGER LAW. His foe was 'Black Gold'—that precious metal [sic] more coveted than the yellow gold the early 49'ers fought and died for, whose power drove men to pillage, to murder, and unjust lynching."

Hatfield is a man among men, a hero of Bunyanesque proportions:

When Jim Hatfield walked into his captain's presence and stood before his desk, the grizzled old frontiersman thought of something he had once seen many years before. Before his eyes drifted the unforgettable picture of a moonlight night in the mountains, with one gaunt crag fanging up against the black sky, and on that crag, etched in silver by the moonlight, a mountain lion, lonely, aloof, head raised, lithe form poised as if to soar away from the solid rock and dare the black depths that yawned beneath.

"All steel and hick'ry and coiled-up chain lightnin'," mused the captain.

(The rather purplish nature of that passage and others are one pointer to Leslie Scott as the author. In those Hatfield's which are indisputably his, in the scores of novels he produced as by Bradford Scott and A. Leslie and under his own name, and in his 80-plus Walt Slade paperback oaters published by Pyramid between 1956 and 1973, there are numerous such lavishly lavender descriptions, some of the more memorable of which you've already had the pleasure of reading in Chapter 6. Oscar Schisgall was a much less verbose, and therefore much less interesting, pulpeteer.)

The characters who help, hinder, and continually try to salivate the Lone Wolf once he arrives in Alamita are a wild and woolly lot. There is Barrel-belly Burks, who runs the Grand Imperial Hotel and who "has warts and no morals...weighs part of a ton and has a voice like a tail-pinched rat"; Sam Sullivan, proprietor of the Glug-Glug Saloon; Miguel Garcia, owner of a "buzzard roost" watering hole in the Mexican quarter; Sheriff Bart Cole, crooked as a dog's hind leg and in the employ of a group of New York capitalists led by an unscrupulous former Alamita miner, Benson Cartwright (no relation to Ben and the boys on the Ponderosa); Muddy Waters, a "monkey-faced hellion and skookum he-wolf," which is to say slug-slammer; Tom Carney, a small ranch owner (the ranch is small, not Tom); Jim Damrock, an old cattle king and father of Rose, who is in love with Tom; a band of outlaws, "the wust gang of sidewinders and horned toads in the hull South-west," led by Black Bender; and yet another dispenser of tarantula juice, Bull Bellows, whose place of business in the outlaw border town of Goromo is called the "Here You Get It" Saloon.

Hatfield's adventures with these and assorted others in Alamita Basin, the surrounding hills, Goromo, and the wilds of Mexico read like a novelization of a '30s movie serial written by Ed Earl Repp. Gunfights, fistfights, and other action sequences not only abound, they virtually stumble over one another; Hatfield gets himself into and out of melodramatic hot water so often he ought to be puckered and parboiled by the final chapter. He is wounded by a drygulcher, nearly drowned in a millrace in a mountain gorge, lassoed and knocked on the head, kidnapped and chained inside an abandoned mine, almost knifed by an allegedly sweet young saloon girl who "danced like a leaf in a vagrant breeze," and nearly salivated, punctured, ventilated, and lead-pizened on half a dozen different occasions.

In addition, he finds time to set a dynamite boobytrap to blow up outlaws who are cutting fences in order to steal cattle, because "the only way to deal with hyderphobia skunks is to wipe 'em out"; save Rose Damrock's life; save Tom Carney's life three times, once from a lynch mob; follow a trail of stolen cattle into the Mexican wilderness; pose as a hyderphobia skunk himself in order to track down Black Bender's hideout, which is located (yes!) in a hidden grotto inside a mountain reached by means of a cave behind a waterfall; discover salt and sulphur springs (by dint of a convenient knowledge of geology from his college days) which tell him that oil—black gold—is what's behind the capitalists' scheme to start a bloody range war so they can gain control of the basin; help dig an oil well, which yields a gusher, which soon turns Alamita into a boom-camp surrounded by derricks and controlled by an outfit called the Great Western Oil Company; vanquish Muddy Waters and Black Bender's gang in a shootout in which "men went down in a storm of lead like bowled over rabbits"; expose Benson Cartwright as the head of the Great Western Oil Company; expose Sheriff Cole as a Cartwright flunky and then fill him full of lead; avoid by the skin of his teeth being blown up in a Cartwright-triggered explosion of one of the derricks; and escape "a flood of fire that rushed down the steep slope like a raging wind" and engulfs Cartwright instead.

Slicker 'n slobbers, no?

All of this frantic and frenetic blather is told in energetic prose dripping with flowery descriptive passages of the sort Leslie Scott specialized in, earthy colloquial dialogue, Texas-style similes and metaphors, and graphic violence that alternates between silly and brutal. The novel's opening paragraph appropriately sets the stage, in more ways than one:

> Sunset over the Sienegas. With a riot of scarlets and golds and purples and trembling amethysts flooding the western sky, as if a drunken god were twirling a rainbow riata over the jagged peaks that spired up to rip the color-drenched clouds to bloody streamers.

Here are a couple of dialogue samples, the first of which is graced by a truly ingenious said substitute:

"Sleep well?" asked Barrel-belly.

> "Shore," Jim told him, "like a bear in a butter tub. Thought I heerd shootin' 'long some time durin' the night, though."
>   "Yuh did," rusty-pumped Barrel-belly.

"Garcia, one more move like that in my direction and I'll slit yore damn neck and shove yore leg through it! So long as I'm workin' for yuh, I'll take orders from yuh, but don'tcha go playin' big skookum he-wolf with me! Hereafter when yuh fill yore hand, play it, and don't try to run a whizzer!"

And a few of the niftier similes:

Before him stretched a long slope dotted with groves and thickets among which the trail wound like a bad-tempered snake through a cactus patch.

Darkness like the inside of a black bull at the bottom of a well at midnight swooped down.

"As a sheriff yuh're about as much good as a mangy last year's hide stuffed with chawed and swallered hay!"

Jim Hatfield went into that cave like a sausage down a houn' dawg's throat.

The tall puncher went into action like a lightning flash through a tub of goose grease.

The man grunted like a hog with a rattlesnake's tail stuck in its throat.

"To chase that seven-foot hellion on a slabsided jughead 'thout a saddle would be jest about as sensible as ridin' the sharp end of a cactus spine after a sore-tailed catamount."

Which brings us, at last, to the bold, stunning, innovative, and casually insane plot ingredient that can be found in no other Western. It occurs while the Lone Wolf is on the trail of the stolen cattle in the Mexican mountains. A shootout ensues when he chances upon the rustlers, forcing Hatfield to take refuge in a cave. The rustlers, wily devils that they are, dynamite the cave entrance, trapping Hatfield inside. ("Now I know jest how a frog feels when he's crawled in a milk jug and somebody's corked it up on him.") He has nowhere to go but deeper into the cave, which leads him down into the depths of the mountain were the air grows warmer and warmer. Could it be that he's entering "the very bowels of a volcano"?

Yes, it could. But not just any old active volcano near the Tex–Mex border, as he soon discovers. In a vast ampitheatre containing a coiling, bubbling lake of molten fire, he comes upon a second awesome spectacle.

Winged and scaled, birdlike and serpentine, a great stone figure crouched against a wall of black rock. Its inscrutable eyes were of reddish quartz and its mouth was the hooked beak of a vulture. Surmounting its feathered headdress fantastically carved in stone was a gleaming crescent of silver. Silently the Ranger stood and gazed at the ghostly form of a god.

"This musta been a old Aztec temple," he mused.

Yes, it must. But the Aztec temple isn't the most amazing thing he encounters in the volcano's bowels—not by half, it isn't. The temple isn't The Ingredient. The Ingredient is—

Giant crabs.

Giant phosphorescent crabs!

GIANT FIGHTING SCREAMING KILLER CRABS!

The depths were swarming with monstrous luminescent forms,

moon-bright, crawling, writhing—claws, feelers and dreadful protruding eyes. Gigantic crabs that lived in holes and under boulders. Aroused by the Ranger's passage through the water, they were swarming toward him. Shuddering with horror, he dashed through the glowing water.

A sharp pain stabbed his thigh. One of the monsters had seized him in viselike claws.

Jim surged forward and broke its grip, and as another of the devilish phosphorescent things rose to the surface directly in front of him he jerked his dripping gun from its holster and struck viciously with the heavy barrel.

The crab, its shell shattered, set up a horrid hoarse screaming and its fellows, perceiving it to be hurt, surged about it with reaching claws and chopping mouths.

Jim plowed madly through the glittering water, cracking shells and breaking claws until the cavern was an inferno of screams and crackling hisses. Behind him the swirls of pale blue light rolled in pursuit.

Reeling, gasping, utterly exhausted, he stumbled on and just as his last strength was flowing from him the water began to shoal. A moment later he struggled through the last shallows and sank panting upon the rock floor. He took a dozen gulping breaths, glanced over his shoulder and swore despairingly.

"The damn things are follerin' me right out onto the land!" he gulped.

Yes, they are. But they're slow, clumsy creatures and the Lone Wolf soon outdistances them and then escapes the volcano by climbing up over the lip of a crater. The giant phosphorescent screaming killer crabs are never seen or heard from again. Nor are they explained, rationalized, or even mentioned again.

Splendiferous ploy. Stroke of utter genius that makes Gene Autry's gunfight with the Muranian superman and his death-dealing raygun in *The Phantom Empire* seem uninspired and insignificant by comparison. Leslie Scott or whoever came up with it has my undying gratitude and an eternal place of honor in the Alternative Hall of Fame.

GUNSMOKE, Clem Colt

As I said in an earlier chapter, Nelson Nye, the prolific Western novelist and authority on quarter horses, was something of a literary Jekyll and Hyde: He could be very, very good and he could also be very, very alternative. Often enough he managed this difficult feat in the same book, and occasionally on the same page—a consequence, perhaps, of the fact that he turned out copy at a white heat. He averaged six novels per annum in the years prior to World War II, and claims to have once written three full-length books in 20 days.

As was the case with many of his contemporaries, Nye had a great fondness for Western vernacular and sometimes overworked it to the point of incomprehensibility. As in this passage from the Clem Colt oater, GUNSLICK MOUNTAIN: "Jake juned around like the seam-squirrels had him. He could not seem to hold his eyes on Sundance; they frittered around like a harried heel fly." Or this one from MULE MAN: "I felt meaner than gar soup thickened with tadpoles, too damned riled to keep a hitch on my lip."

He also did himself proud, alternatively and otherwise, with his penchant for colorful manipulation (sometimes strangulation) of the English language. Similes and metaphors abound in his work, as do inspired synonyms and verbs of his own manufacture (such as "juned" in the example above). Such rampant experimentation often worked; just as often it didn't. Here are two sentences from the same chapter of GUNSLICK MOUNTAIN, the first a sample of Good Nye and the second a sample of Alternative Nye:

> Jake...was sunk beyond the reach of threats, a man buried deep in the debris of his own scheming.

> The crash of the shot gagged the night with its clamor.

GUNSMOKE, the first of more than 20 titles published under his Clem Colt pseudonym, is atypical Nye in that it has a West Texas setting, rather than the Arizona milieu of most of his novels. The hero is young Red Lawler, sheriff of Pecos, a "sleepy little cowtown sprawled in slumbrous lethargy near the banks of a mud-brown river," and the plot is a standard lawdog-versus-outlaw-crew bang-banger, the crew in this case led by a bushwhacking killer who leaves notes signed with the word "Justice." Along with the usual quota of gun-soirées and hair-breadth escapes, there is a considerable amount of what Nye himself characterized as "redeeming humor of the droll, wry variety." It is that redeeming humor, or rather a particular type of it, that warrants GUNSMOKE's inclusion here.

Red Lawler's sidekick is a gent named Pony George Kasta, who has "a dried-apple countenance" and a drooping, straw-colored mustache. After the fashion of Andrew A. Griffin's Johnny Forty-five, Pony George fancies himself a poet. He is constantly giving birth to "another of those four-line atrocities which he pridefully labeled 'poetry,'" heralding each new verse with a "series of grunts, groans and salty ejaculations" and then, after inflicting same on Red Lawler, patting himself on the back by declaiming, "Gosh—ain't that a pistol!" Nearly a score of these verses are reproduced in the pages of GUNSMOKE, each one part and parcel of an episodic poem Pony George is constructing entitled "The Ballad of Kyote Cal."

It is no exaggeration to say that Pony George and Nelson Nye are even more formidable alternative rhymemakers than Johnny Forty-five and Andrew A. Griffin. As evidence, I offer some of the choicer stanzas:

> A yarn I'll spin that's full o' sin,
> It's a tale both old an' new—
> A saga of times when men was bad
> An' women was bold as brew!

> This ornery Cal was the sneakin' pal
> What stole his pard's best dame;
> She was a busy, hustlin' skirt
> Thet sang in the Golden Flame.

> One night at the Flame, Cal an' his dame
> Was havin' a damn mean row—
> When in through the door stepped a tall slim gent
> With his hat pulled low on his brow.

> One hand, long an' lean, clung close to his Colt;
> As he chuckled right nasty an' grim—
> "Jest lissen tuh me, yuh dirty Piute;
> Thet dame yuh been neckin's my bim!"

> Cal whirled around quick, an' he sez "Looky here,
> Pilgrim, yo're headin' fer hell—
> I don't give a damn if yo're mean as a mule;
> It's time someone sounded yore knell!"

> "Oh yeah?" says the stranger. "Yuh son of a Chink!
> Get yore paws up an' keep 'em right still—
> Don't gimme no sass, yuh mangy kyote,
> 'Cause it's you thet I'm pinin' tuh drill!"

> Swift his narrow-eyed glare flashed round like a curse,
> As he looked for Kyote Cal's dame—
> She stood there by the bar, with her hand on a knife,
> An' her charms standin' out like a flame.

> 'Tis a saga of sorrow, a tale bold but true,
> That yuh've heard of ol' Kyote Cal—
> An' the moral this sage has tried tuh drive in, is
> *Don't be a fool for a gal!*

Gosh. Ain't that moral a pistol?

THE OUTLAWS OF CAJA BASIN, Jackson Cole

The jacket blurb on this Jackson Cole powdersmoker, which stars Brad "Brazos" Kennedy in lieu of Jim Hatfield, begins with the statement: "Now and then there is offered to the lover of Western novels, a story so out of the ordinary in its richness of thrills, pictured by a master hand, that it is an open sesame to the hearts of red-blooded Americans."

Bullpoop.

BLACK GOLD is out of the ordinary in its richness of thrills; this gun-roaring tale of modern bushwhackers and kidnappers running amok on the Turkey Track Range would be just another '30s Texas skirt job if it weren't for its first two chapters. Those opening chapters *were* pictured by a master hand, fortunately, so its open sesame is not to the hearts of red-blooded Americans but to the doors of the Alternative Hall of Fame.

Leslie Scott and/or Oscar Schisgall may have written the balance of OUTLAWS OF CAJA BASIN, but if either man perpetrated the first 29 pages he was blind drunk or suffering from a severe attack of the seam squirrels. More likely it was a fledgling wannabe who was allowed, for some obscure reason, to briefly flap his fictional wings. Nepotism, perhaps, the individual being a poor relation of an editor or publisher. By the time his functional illiteracy was discovered, and he was chucked out of the bunkhouse never to be heard from again, it was too late for Scott or Schisgall to do much except finish the novel and hope that nobody paid close attention to its initial 10,000 words. The only other explanation I can come up with is that an imp of the perverse—the ghost of Bulwer-Lytton, say—got his otherworldly dew-clams on a perfectly competent (by pulp standards) manuscript after it had been accepted for publication and gleefully and maniacally screwed up Chapters 1 and 2.

In any case, those first 29 pages are a lopsided monument to fractured English. Only in the mystery field, in the works of such alternative greats as Florence Mae Pettee, will the discerning reader find butchery of such magnitude.

> He was beginning to wonder if he would have enough [clothing] left to cover himself with if he ever did stumble on some friendly cabin for which he was looking. It would suit him much better if he could run into an unused one, which would be all for which he could hope in the higher ground.

> Presently he struck an old cattle trail, followed it until it began to wind around the foothills of a rise.
> Then silence, unbroken and drowsy, held sway over the ridge once more. Only, when the breeze halted for a breath of space, just the faint scent of herb-scented tobacco drifting to Kennedy's acute sense of smell let him know, aside from the first sounds he had heard, that the gap possessed other human habitation than himself.

There was something furtive and underhand in the slithering manner in which those feet had scampered.

Brad Kennedy's lean face, though stained by sun and wind, smudged by blind-baggage [train] travel, and muddied from his last night's encounter with an obstreperous stream and with no chance as yet to remove its traces, was not of that weather-cured, deep-dyed hue one instinctively notices as the copyright of the Southwestern man.

He lifted his brawny arm, and a single blow from it sent the boy sprawling into the dust of the road, shooting through the car door like a catapult.

A bullet had found its way to some portion of Brad's anatomy that was resenting it.

He tossed aside the buzzing noise in his ears, the sickness and faintness, and staggered on...hurling his useless weapon from him like a man gone berserk and catapulted himself at the girl's manhandler with a Tarzan roar.

And Brad Kennedy's vision went out in a burst like fire-glare laid upon a world that reeled in a devil's hornpipe. The sinking sun vaulted halfway across the sky and struck him.

My best guess is that the remainder of the book was written by Oscar Schisgall, since it lacks the distinctive purple hue and Lone Star patter that mark Leslie Scott's work. But you should not think, no matter which professional hand penned the final 227 pages, that those pages are totally lacking in alternative pleasures.

She said eagerly: "I haven't thanked you yet for—everything. I do, I do thank you, Mr.——"

"Brazos," Kennedy answered bluntly. "Not Mister—just Brazos."

She laughed lightly, the sound coursing through Brad like little tinkles of highland bells. "Brazos! Why, that's the name of a river! It's always sounded to me like moonlight and ripples and the tinkle of guitars and soft, bright things, like Mexican girls' laughter...."

The guns in each of his hands began drumming their own scarlet *rafale*. In answer came red flashes and snarling slugs from Quamon's crew as some of them turned in surprise at this new challenge to their rear.

BLACK CREEK BUCKAROO, Anson Piper (Anthony M. Rud)

As the reader who has delved into SON OF GUN IN CHEEK will recall, Anthony Rud was a highly regarded (by me, anyway) writer of alternative mysteries as well as of alternative Westerns. His "full-fledged, card-carrying supersleuth," Jigger Masters, hero of several pulp stories and such cracked novel masterpieces as HOUSE OF THE DAMNED and THE STUFFED MEN, is a first-magnitude star in the firmament of loony heroes.

A Chicago native, Rud began writing shortly after his graduation from Dartmouth in 1914, and over the next 25 years contributed short stories, novelettes, and serials in a variety of fields—jungle adventure, mystery, Western, science fantasy, horror—to a variety of pulp magazines, among them *Argosy, Lariat, Thrilling Wonder, Detective Fiction Weekly, Weird Tales* (where his best-known story, "Ooze," was originally published in 1923), and even *Black Mask* in its early years. He also worked as an editor on both *Adventure* and *Detective Story* from the late '30s until his death in 1942, just shy of his 50th birthday.

Of Rud's nine novels, five are Westerns. The first two, THE LAST GRUBSTAKE and THE SENTENCE OF THE SIX GUN, were pulp serials brought out in book form by Doubleday, Page in the '20s, as part of their "Pocket Copyright" line of pulp reprints (a line similar to Street & Smith's "Popular Copyrights" Chelsea House books, though distributed for the most part in dime-novel-style paperback editions). Anson Piper made his pseudonymous debut in BLACK CREEK BUCKAROO in 1941, a rather surprising link in Morrow's well-regarded chain of action Westerns. The remaining two Pipers, THE PAINTED GHOST and BLUEBONNET RANGE, were both published in England in 1946 and have no U.S. editions.

In both his crime yarns and his horse operas, Rud specialized in eccentric (and eccentrically named) characters, in vastly improbable situations that contain all sorts of mismatched elements, and as Cussemout Crandall demonstrated in Chapter 7, in some of the most originative screwball dialogue ever to spring from a fictioneer's imagination. BLACK CREEK BUCKAROO is loaded with bits and pieces of his unique brand of nonsense. Allegedly set in the Texas

Panhandle (Rud's Texas, while different from John Creasey's version, is no less a fantasyland), the story has as its hero Breck Wilson, "foreman pro tem of the wealthy Rafter T, and for six years an
unquestioned top hand with horse, rope, six-shooter, rifle—or
fists."

Breck dreams of owning his own ranch and has his eye on an
old trapper's cabin near Hondo Creek. But nesters have taken over
the cabin (or are the interlopers really nesters?), and by the end of
the first chapter they have blown the place to fragments in a dynamite explosion that loudly says, "Grrrrrooooouuuummmm!"
That's when things *really* start to happen to and because of Breck,
who "jest bulls ahead and does things irregardless, like a dose of
croton oil goin' down a sow's throat."

Breck's adventures include trouble with nesters, rustlers, dead
cows, a bunch of Kansas pumpkins, milk goats, an emerald
brooch, mules, Indians, night riders, lead-slingers, a mandolin
tune called "Rackamaw Jig," and the U.S. Cavalry.

Among the individuals he favors and locks horns with are she-
birds named Mary Landon ("a plumb tinsel angel"), Nettie Royce
(a.k.a. Lady Button Eyes, who calls him "the blue-eyed menace"),
Federal Court Judge Big-Horn Bascom, a salt-cured ranch cook
with the handle of Rooty Tuohy, a Piute Indian brave called Little
Smoke, two Piute squaws known as Missus Hippy (a.k.a. Rains-All-
Day) and Danger at Night, cowboys and ranchers named Buff
Orpington, Windigo Rains, Pogey Mallen, and the Hassayampa
Kid, a snakehunter dubbed Sibby Sawtell, an overstuffed ex-
barkeep whose moniker is Egg-Head (because he has "a face like
an omelet, an' a head shaped like the rest of the egg"), an outlaw
known as Romero the Mexican, Nick St. John, "the high-priced
killer of Tascosa," two vicious gunhawks called Twenty-Mile Mit-
chell and Peanuts Bagg, and Old Clint Rafferty, owner of the Rafter
T, whose favorite expressions are "Moses on a miser'ble mountain"
and "By the whiskers of whistlin' Willyum."

The action, much of it to the accompaniment of Tompkins-
style sound effects *(Wham! Crash! Tinkle! Bong!)*, takes place in
such locales as Punkinhead Range, Pawnbroker Ranch, Star Sten-

cil Ranch, J Up and J Down Ranch, Dogey Coulee, and the No Snakes Saloon.

If I were to attempt to sort all of these disparate components into a coherent synopsis, it would take me several pages and even then it wouldn't do the proceedings justice. This is another of those books that have to be read in all their magnificent lunacy to be properly appreciated. What I will do is to provide a few more specimens of Rud's Western pod-creature dialogue.

This is how Breck Wilson talks:

"Hey, you chunkers! Gimme my pants! Who's glommed on to my new corduroys? Who's the ranny that limped away with 'em, huh?"

This is how Rafter T cowhands talk:

"Hoo-oo! Dingle-dang it all! Somebody's swiped my Sunday shirt, the crimson silk one! By gummus an' gran'ma, I'll chaw his ears down to the roots!"

This is how Old Clint Rafferty talks:

"Hell's bells an' boomalacka bunions! Breck, didja think I'd waste m' time and brains workin' out a scheme like this, if'n it wasn't a good one, a dinger? Huh? Now, don't go to imaginin' re-mote possibilities, an' pilin' horseradish on my plan."

"Moses on a miser'ble mud mountain! I've helled around some, I'll admit, as a younker. But by damn and hell's whiskers, I'm respectable now, I am. I'm too dang old to finagle around an' play Dan Cupid in the love affairs of a dingle-danged punkin' vine!"

And this is how Rooty Tuohy, the ranch cook, talks:

"Green River gravy bowl!" exclaimed Rooty, his eyes widening.

"By the snaggle-tooth of Laughin' Lulu, you sure got lucky!"

"My gawsh! I'll have to sorta enlarge the kitchens, sorta. Or mebbe you'll build me a special pie cookhouse, Clint? Lessee, a good big punkin'll make four pies. Four times one hundred and forty-four— oh gawsh, I can't multiplicate that far. But I'm here to state, it's one hellious-bellious hoodle of punkin pie!"

"Oh, it's you, huh? Well, why'n the name of whem-gubblin' gruxes of Mongreymoul didn'tcha say so?"

The Bird Cage, Lynton Wright Brent

Sexy Westerns such as Lust Gallops into the Desert and The Furious Passion of the Laughing Gun were not Brent's only contributions to the genre. He also wrote traditional shoot-'em-ups, mainly for a short-lived Southern California publisher, Powell Books, after the demise of his own Brentwood Publishing Co. Powell (1969–70, requiescat in pace) brought out dozens of mystery, Western, science-fiction, and romance novels and short-story collections during its brief life; among the Westerns were six collections of four novelettes per book that carried Brent's byline and had such titles as Apache Tomahawk, Outlaw Village, and Thunder of the Arrows. These are splendidly awful. As is a Powell mystery novel by Brent, Death of a Detective. As is his purported "documentary on violence and crime in the Movie Capital of the World," Hollywood Crime & Scandal. Come to think of it, nothing that Lynton Wright Brant published is anything but splendidly awful.

But his magnum opus is The Bird Cage, which as noted previously was also his first novel. Published in 1945 by Dorrance & Company of Philadelphia, a vanity press, its dust-jacket blurb says inaccurately, "Here is the first novel ever written about Tombstone, Arizona," and goes on to declaim, also fibbing shamelessly, "It is the thrilling story of a theatrical troupe that came by stagecoach to open this once wild and reckless mining town's historic Bird Cage Theatre in 1881.... A book pulsating with violent love and living—one you will wish to read and to own."

C. L. Sonnichsen, in From Hopalong to Hud, held an opinion of the novel that approximates mine. He called it "an astonishing fictional concoction," and went on to state that it "has small merit as a novel. It sounds like East Lynne or one of the old melodramas moved to the Southwest, where the superheated emotions and overblown style are much less tolerable than they would have been elsewhere."

Here is Sonnichsen's capsule summary of the plot, which is better than any I could offer:

Tombstone's famous theatre is about to open, and Donna Drew is coming with her company from New York to present *The Westerner*. Donna is a ravishing redhead who has every able-bodied male in Tombstone drooling, especially Peter Crawley, professional gambler and impresario; Matthew Prane of the P-Bar-B Ranch; and Matthew's partner, Steve Brammer. Prane himself comes from stage people who were killed and robbed by a gang of desperadoes...many years before. Matt [is] obsessed by the idea of killing the murderers. As the story opens, he has disposed of four of them and is looking for the fifth and last.

   The show opens and is a failure [because no one involved] knows anything about the West. Matthew steps in, rewrites the play, becomes the leading man, and takes the show to New York, unaware that Brammer has raped Donna in her dressing room and is the fifth man he is looking for. Successful in the East, the troupe comes back for a Tombstone triumph and to a showdown between Matthew and Steve. Donna finds that she is carrying Steve's baby, but nobody seems to be unhappy about that at the end.

The main story line and various subplots are even more of a hodgepodge than Sonnichsen's summary indicates. But it is Brent's sterling prose that makes THE BIRD CAGE the triumph it is. Just how overblown and melodramatic is his style in this maiden effort? Behold his descriptive powers and attempts at characterization:

The warm night-wind swept down from the Dragoon Mountains as though to flaunt confirmation of Nature's acknowledged capriciousness. In any other part of the wild and reckless Territory of Arizona, this open sesame to vigorous, healthful life would have belonged to Spring.

His sharp blue eyes were alive with dancing pebbles of fire, akin to sparks leaping from a blacksmith's busy anvil, which gave him the vigorous, expectant look of the man, spirit-starved, who has just discovered where to find his particular kind of coveted mental grub.

   Matthew Prane for ten years had endured the agony of a devastating thought, until his brain had cried out violently for relief. The torturing urge to commit compensative murder had demanded an avocative thought, something to relieve his brain of such gruesome tension.

Matthew's heavy black eyebrows drew together in a desperate effort to invent a clever rebuttal.

The old feeling of slime, snakes, returned to his mind and physical senses.

Something inside Lily Palmer rolled over and rammed against her feelings.

"The Dragoons are so much——" The broken utterance lifted strength to her mouth, and she swallowed sub-consciously, as though some kindly creature had just furbished her soul with the clean medicine of the earth—the good earth; the solid earth which supplied a foundation for her feet.

Behold his action sequences:

During the reception of felling blows, Matthew thought of Donna Drew—and he was not unhappy.... He was delighted over the added power the thought of her allotted him. The memory of her surged through his veins; and he felt the force of it as his fists drove hammer-like. His body was painfully bruised, but now his spirit soared high over the heads of his attackers.

Suddenly, as he lay prone, his rifle bounced to his shoulder [and] he fired.

Both men were sweating profusely, despite the fact that the penetrating Arizona sun was slipping down behind the Whetstone mountain quietly, neutrally....

Sensing that his strength for combative action would not exist much longer, and wracking his brain for the animal cunning he needed now to end this struggle victoriously for himself, Matthew at last left his face unguarded. He received several penetrating blows thereafter.... But he rallied every ounce of available strength, every spark of viciousness, every iota of animal nature within him —and pounded with his big right slugger.

Behold his dialogue:

"I know you well enough," she told him, "to know that you only play one woman at a time. And when you make a change—the other woman is through."

"That's right, my dear."

"Then—I am through?"

"That's right, Lily."

"Just like that, huh? Lordy! Crawley, you are worse than a Gila monster! You are worse than Satan! You are the filth of the earth!"

Crawley was grinning amusedly at her scathing metaphors.

"A man's nature, my dear," said the gambler, "requires that occasionally he have a change of venison."

"I'm Steve—and yo're Donna! Yo're beautiful, and I'm rugged. And life is what yuh make of it—if yuh got sense enough tuh recognize a good roundup when it comes."

"To hell with everything," she muttered incoherently.

Crawley chuckled ruggedly. "Traggit's getting rustler's pneumonia," he remarked to Steve. "His courage is freezing."

"Justice," Nellie mused, "does not always fall on the right side of the pasture."

"She's too beautiful to be alive," Crawley murmured. "An ace in the world's beauty-deck!"

Aces in the alternative-Western deck—that's THE BIRD CAGE and Lynton Wright Brent.

THE BORDER EAGLE, Walker A. Tompkins

It's only fitting that our final Alternative Western Hall of Fame entry be another of Two-Gun Tompkins' quintessential bang-bangers. THE BORDER EAGLE was his first for Phoenix Press and was based on, or perhaps lifted wholly or in part from, a series of stories he contrived for *Wild West Weekly* under the pseudonym Philip F. Deere; it immediately established him as an ace ramrod on the Phoenix spread. Along with BORDER BONANZA, it ranks as his most memorable achievement.

The titular hero, whose real handle is Trigger Trenton, is a U.S. Marshal who "joined the forces of law with only one objective in mind—to locate his brother, Jack Trenton, or failing in that, to avenge his brother's death. [His] feats of derring had won for him, inside of eighteen flaming, daredevil months, the title of the 'Border Eagle,' loved by every man, woman, and child in five law-abiding states." He has "a pair of massive shoulders, as square as a block of granite [and] lean legs encased in Cheyenne-style chaps with leather tie conchas." He wears blunt-roweled spurs buckled on kangaroo-leather boots, and carries a pair of ivory-butted .45s in "shiny holsters, basket woven, thonged at the muzzle ends." A flowing red bandanna is the only spot of color in his otherwise solemn (for a Tompkins' protagonist) costume. All in all, an impressive figure—until he opens his mouth. When he makes that mistake, this is the sort of thing that comes out:

"I'll be teetotally danged."

"Yore in a shaved ace o' takin' a one-way ticket to blazes, Mex!"

"Which same words was perzactly the booger talk this Soldavo skunk was makin', a couple of ticks afore he took a ride down the slick skids to blazes."

The story opens, typically, in a thunder of angel makers during which gunfight Trigger Trenton salivates Pepe Soldavo, "the most brutal killer along the Arizona border." Shortly afterward, while fleeing from Pepe's boss, Demon Horne, "notorious smuggling chief," a.k.a. "the king of all smuggling kings," the Border Eagle—in a Tompkins masterstroke of improbable coincidence—stumbles upon the skeleton of his long-lost brother, half hidden under "a carpet of dead thistle poppies" in a badlands canyon. (He knows the skeleton is his brother's because he finds "balanced over the slot between two rib-bones" a U.S. Marshal's badge identical to his own.) A dying message fingernail-scratched into rock on a nearby cave wall identifies Jack's slayer as one Baldy Cook.

Vowing bloody vengeance, Trenton makes his way into Suicide Valley and begins his hunt for this Baldy Cook jasper. Before long, his path crosses those of such individuals as:

⅄ Max Sumpter, owner of the SV Ranch, who says things like "Honin' to rent yore rope, eh? Waal, we ain't got no places open.

Yuh kin bed down for the night, though. But come mornin', I'll
have to ask yuh to rattle yore hocks thither, buckaroo."

❦ Texanna Sumpter, Max's "starry-eyed girl," with whom the Border Eagle is soon smitten—so smitten that her father is later
prompted to observe that Trigger Trenton is "the fust feller I ever
seen as could fall in love with a woman, give her a kiss, an' be off
on a six-gun trail, all in the same breath!"

❦ Hob Lipe, wearer of a gunny-sack apron around his "gorilla
middle" that instantly marks him as the ranch cook, and described
as having "a thick, shaven head, as knobby as a lump of rock [and]
a pair of stern eyes as black as raw gunpowder—cold and evil. The
man's nose was thick-lobbed and twisted to one side by the same
snarl which pulled the lips into a slanting red line across the blue-
jowled face. The man's grimy white shirt was stuffed with muscles,
and a carpet of hair showed at the open throat."

❦ Demon Horne, something of an evil vision in black and white:
black silk shirt, white leather vest with ornate black trim, black-
and-white batwing chaps, white cartridge belt containing black-
butted .45s, a black Stetson hat. Inexplicably, his sacklike mask is
of blue silk—something of a lapse in sartorial harmony, but then
what can you expect from an evil smuggling chief?

❦ Poison Fang, notorious Apache outlaw, who passes such re-
marks as "Keep um heap still, Sumpter! Pull um mitt out o' them
papers. You might have um shoot-iron cached in thar."

❦ Kink Nibless, sickly-faced gambler, who chin-gabs thusly: "I
been hopin' our sticks would drift together ag'in, you salty young
sprout! The Border Eagle, eh? Wal, hard luck has laid a nit in yore
feathers, this deal. Better be gittin' down on yore prayer bones,
Trenton. Yore goin' to git yores!"

❦ The Mummy, a dried-up old Indian who guards a place called
the Haunted Pueblo that was built by "ancient Zunis."

❦ Hopi Joe, a dried-up old Indian desert rat who ends up dead in
a well full of "pizened minerals" known as the Well of Doom.

♈ Arana the Spider, a bulldog-jawed vinegaroon who opines: "Afore that Trenton hombre ever dabs his loop on Horne, his hide'll be curin' under a cloud o' buzzards."

♈ Pablo Germez, devil-faced Mexican bandit, who is blown away by Demon Horne because he says in a cowardly whimper, "*Pero, señor*—no! NO! Thees Border Eagle—he ees keel me! Do not send Pablo to be keeled by thees Border Eagle!"

Action scenes involving these and other individuals are strung together like exploding firecrackers (a simile Two-Gun himself might have jabbed up). Smoke-wagons roar in Suicide Valley, in the Sunblaze Mountains, in Devil's Gorge, near Tombstone Peak, at the edge of Goathoof Basin: *Whinng! Crrash! Bam-bam-bam! Bang-bang-bang-bang! Brrang-bram! Bam-slam!* There is an attempt to croak Trigger Trenton by feeding him poisoned coffee, which our sensitive hero circumvents by deliberately and cold-bloodedly feeding it to a cat instead. There is another attempt to croak Trenton by tossing him into a pit filled with rattlesnakes. And finally there is a climactic duel between the Border Eagle and Demon Horne, in which the king of all smuggling kings is unmasked and our hero finds himself staring in amazement into the face of none other than Hob Lipe, the bald S V Ranch cook ("Baldy Cook"—get it?).

> Trenton's brain worked faster than his dazed muscles during that split clock tick when the two men stooped to pick up their six-guns from underfoot.
>
> The Eagle's lightning flash of memory covered back to the time when he had first come to Suicide Valley. Hob Lipe, who had faked a crippled leg as part of his disguise, had in reality been the great Demon Horne himself!
>
> No one would suspect a ranch cook of being Demon Horne. [No one except any reader with an IQ above 50.] Yet from the kitchen of Max Sumpter's ranch, the shaven-skulled Hob Lipe had directed the greatest smuggling ring on the border, using his days off to visit his hide-out lair on Tombstone Peak.

And a lot of days off he took, too, once Trigger Trenton showed up in Suicide Valley.

The Border Eagle finally perforates Horne/Lipe with the same bullet Horne/Lipe used to salivate Trenton's brother. But not before there is considerably more gunplay *(Brrum! Brrrt! Spang! Brr-rom!)* and Trigger is forced to seek refuge behind "a silvery-gray hedge of *ignota.*"

Ignota hedges, a.k.a. ignota brush, turn up elsewhere in THE BORDER EAGLE, and in a couple of Tompkins' other Phoenix Westerns as well. A typical Arizona border-country plant? Well, no, not hardly. Two-Gun's research (if in fact he did much research in those halcyon pre-war days) sometimes failed him, yielding bizarre as well as inaccurate results.

Ignota, you see, is neither a hedge nor a bushy plant.

It's a type of moss.

Walker Tompkins not only invented the world's first rhinestone cowboy; he invented the one and only Incredible Shrinking Buckaroo, who was able to avoid hot lead by crawling behind a patch of moss!

She came over to the bed, looking fine and sweet in a calico dress with her auburn hair fluffed out over her shoulders, and sat beside him. He reached out, took her hand, held it tightly in his own big calloused one. There were no words between them and none needed. Her eyes told him everything he needed to know, and her lips confirmed it seconds later.

There would be no more fiddlefooted drifting for Jim Glencannon, no more lonely nights beside a string of long and lonely trails. He knew at last what it was he wanted, what he had always wanted deep down inside. And now that he had it, he was never going to let it go.

Laurie's hand would remain clasped in his for the rest of their days. —William Jeffrey (Bill Pronzini and Jeffrey Wallmann), DUEL AT GOLD BUTTES

10. Hand in Hand into the Sunset

The final chapters of bang-bang Westerns, once the powder-smoke cleared and the smoke-poles were tucked into leather, were generally reserved for mop-up explanations and the tying off of at least some loose ends, and for a touch of romance. The hero either opted to maintain a meaningful relationship with his horse and rode off alone into the sunset, or he decided to settle down with his lady love and the two of them walked off together, hand and hand into the sunset. Occasionally a novel would end on a humorous note; more often the last few lines were paeans to sentimentality, meant to leave the action-saturated reader with a smile on his lips and a tear in his eye.

It seems appropriate, then, the old prospector being a sentimental soul himself (as witness the ending lines of DUEL AT GOLD BUTTES above), that this final chapter be devoted to a selection of the more stirring closing paragraphs in alternative Western fiction. Your heart is hard, indeed, if these fadeouts don't leave *you* with a smile on your lips and a tear in your eye...

Terry nodded. "I'd love it, Stephen," she whispered, and their lips met as the crowd made way for the doctor.

Matty nudged old Hamp Carter and made a wry face. "Ain't that jest too sweet fer words, Sheriff?" he said. "Beats shucks how a woman'll swear up an' down she wouldn't marry the best man on earth, then turn right aroun' an' kiss one smack in front uh everybody. An' no matter how bad a feller is shot up, he's still got enough taw left in his gizzard tuh make love!" (Ed Earl Repp, GUN HAWK)

"I haven't asked Caroline—yet. But it's something I aim to do just the minute you hombres leave us alone."

A faint flush crossed the girl's face, but she looked at the gathered men squarely, and nodded. As they grinned in understanding and drew away, Utah's arms reached up, and Caroline Bannister leaned down to meet him. As their lips met, a little form on velvet wings flitted in the opened door, circled the pair once, and settled on Utah's shoulder, as if giving him benediction. (Galen C. Colin, DRY GULCH)

"So you knew all the time where she was at, eh?" Cross-Draw shook his head and scowled. "You certainly are one steamin' Romeo—I expect we better git you outa here 'fore yore flamin' ardor sets the place afire! The idea of you leavin' that nice upstandin' gal all tied up an'——"

"Shucks," murmured Potent soothingly. "She was safe enough. Trouble with you fellas is yuh don't sabe the feminine character. Sure," he nodded, raising a hand for quiet—"like enough she *did* do a heap of frettin'; prob'ly got shivers all over her spinal column. But what of it? *Them's women's joys!* She'll be countin' that a *real experience.* An' when I come wadin' through the powdersmoke t' save her—Shucks! Jest figger it out." (Clem Colt, CENTER-FIRE SMITH)

She seized his hand that was about her waist and squeezed it.

"Yes," she murmured. "And now your vision has come true. But we mustn't let ourselves forget—we must be practical, too. I was reading some lines last night. They said:

> 'In a wife's lap as in a grave
> Men's airy motions mix with the earth.' "

"Sure, that's right," said Steve. "But—with you beside me it'll be *such* an earth. I'll have an angel at the gate. It'll be paradise." (George B. Rodney, THE SECO BONANZA)

"I know now, Gayle," she whispered in the Corporal's ear. "Lenore's a secret service woman, and your sister Frances—Hilda Garfield—is one too. Confess up—you stubborn Mountie!"

"Well, Mona," smiled Gayle, with a flashing return of his old debonair spirit, "we Mounted Police, and government secret service operatives working with the Mounted, reveal ourselves only to our own members. So I guess you'll have to sign up also. Do you think you could raise courage enough to join the matrimonial Force as Mrs. Corporal Conroy?"

"I'll—I'll take the oath, Gayle," Mona promised gaily. (Samuel Alexander White, THE CODE OF THE NORTHWEST)

The women dried their eyes and waved again and again. Joy turned and responded to their Godspeed with kisses tossed from her fingertips.

"May their trail always be through the sunshine," murmured Stone.

At the very edge of the timber both Ladd and Joy turned to wave once more. Then the trees swallowed them.

Ladd, as he looked at his slim, gallant wife-to-be, said something he had said once before.

"Girl, if you only knew how I loved you, you'd curl right up in a spasm."

Again Joy laughed in lilting, burbling happiness. And the heart of her lifted up and up until it seemed to float among the sun-drenched tips of the trees. (L. P. Holmes, THE LAW OF KYGER GORGE)

"Look at him coming with his head up and his shoulders back, Betty," Martha Titus chuckled. "He's got a smile on his face like the wave on a pail of slop, and still his lower lip's all jammed out. He's getting himself ready not to take 'No' for his answer, and I bet he don't have to. Betty Mayne, don't you stand there with your eyes like stars and dare to tell me you don't know what Mesa Malone is coming for!"

"I know!" the girl cried happily.

And she was right. (James P. Olsen, POWDERSMOKE PADDY)

She smiled too, then—sunshine through rain. He had taken her hands. She asked huskily: "Will—will you promise me something, Buzz?"

"I reckon so. What is it you want to ask of me?"

"Promise me you won't ever play that—that terrible music again."

He sobered quickly, told her earnestly, "I hope it won't ever be necessary for me to play it again. I've never been a gunfighter by choice, Boots. I hate the very thought of gun music."

They stood there like that, gazing steadily at each other for a moment, and deep understanding flowed between those two pairs of eyes. On impulse he drew her to him and kissed her tenderly. She smiled at him again—wistfully, happily this time—then hand in hand they walked toward the sunset and into town. (Tex Holt, THE LAWLESS TRAIL)

Bibliography

Novels

Adams, Stuart. RANGE WAR IN SQUAW VALLEY. New York: Hillman Curl, 1939.

Anders, Webb. SADDLE 'N RIDE. London: Scion, 1952.

Baker, A. A. A NOOSE FOR THE MARSHAL. Canoga Park, Calif.: Major Books, 1977.

Ballenger, Dean W. GUNSLINGER JUSTICE. Canoga Park, Calif.: Major Books, 1976.

Brent, Lynton Wright. THE BIRD CAGE. Philadelphia: Dorrance, 1945.

———. THE FURIOUS PASSION OF THE LAUGHING GUN. Hollywood, Calif.: Brentwood, 1965.

———. LUST GALLOPS INTO THE DESERT. Hollywood, Calif.: Brentwood, 1965.

———. PASSIONATE PERIL AT FORT TOMAHAWK. Hollywood, Calif.: Brentwood, 1965.

Brooker, Clark. FIGHT AT SUN MOUNTAIN. New York: Ballantine, 1957.

Byrne, Jack. GUNSWIFT. New York: Doubleday, 1941.

Claussen, W. Edmunds. REBELS ROUNDUP. New York: Abelard Press, 1952.

———. RUSTLERS OF SLABROCK. New York: Phoenix Press, 1946.

Coburn, Walt. BORDER TOWN. New York: Belmont, 1967.

Cody, Al. HANGMAN'S COULEE. New York: Dodd, Mead, 1951.

Cole, Jackson. BLACK GOLD. New York: Caslon, 1936

———. LONE-STAR LAW. New York: M. S. Mill, 1939.

———. THE OUTLAWS OF CAJA BASIN. New York: G. H. Watt, 1934.

———. RIDERS OF THE RIMROCK TRAIL. New York: Gateway, 1942.

———. TEXAS MANHUNT. New York: Pyramid, 1955.

Colin, Galen C. DRY GULCH. New York: Phoenix Press, 1942.

Colt, Clem. CENTER-FIRE SMITH. New York: Phoenix Press, 1942.

———. GUNSLICK MOUNTAIN. New York: Arcadia House, 1945.

Colt, Clem. Gunsmoke. New York: Greenberg, 1938.

———. Guns of Horse Prairie. New York: Phoenix Press, 1943

———. Tough Company. New York: Dodd, Mead, 1952.

Craigie, Hamilton. The Ranch of the Raven. New York: Phoenix Press, 1935.

Culley, Christopher. McCoy of the Ranges. London: Philip Allan, 1936.

Cullum, Ridgwell. The bull Moose. Philadelphia: Lippincott, 1931.

Cutter, Tom. Tracker #5: The Oklahoma Score. New York: Avon, 1984.

Ellis, Wesley. Lone Star and the Aztec Treasure. New York: Jove, 1993.

———. Lone Star and the Hardrock Payoff. New York: Jove, 1981.

———. Lone Star and the Phantom Gunman. New York: Jove, 1987.

Elston, Allan Vaughan. Come Out and Fight! New York: Doubleday, 1941.

Ernenwein, Leslie. Bullet Breed. New York: McBride, 1946.

Floren, Lee. Cottonwood Pards. New York: Phoenix Press, 1944.

Fonville, John. Where the Big Gun Rides. Clovis, Calif.: Vega Books, 1964.

Garth, Will. Lawless Guns. New York: Dodge, 1937.

Gast, Kelly P. The Last Stage from Opal. New York: Doubleday, 1978.

Gooden, Arthur Henry. Smoke Tree Range. New York: Kinsey, 1936.

Grinstead, J. E. Guardians of the Range. New York: Dodge, 1939.

Gunn, Tom. Painted Post Gunplay. New York: Messner, 1937.

———. Painted Post Rustlers. New York: Messner, 1938.

Hoffman, W. D. Gun-Johnnies of Texas. New York: Phoenix Press, 1945.

Holt, Tex. The Lawless Trail. New York: Gateway, 1940.

Holmes, L. P. The Law of Kyger Gorge. New York: Greenberg, 1936.

Jeffrey, William. Duel at Gold Buttes. New York: Leisure, 1981.

Johnstone, William. Trail of the Mountain Men. New York: Zebra, 1987.

Joscelyn, Archie. GUNS OF LOST VALLEY. New York: Phoenix Press, 1940.

———. THE SAWBONES OF DESOLATE RANGE. New York: Phoenix Press, 1941.

Kane, Jack. BUZZARD BAIT. New York: Avalon, 1977.

Kennard, Oscar. TIMBER LINE. London: Curtis Warren, 1952.

Knight, Kim. NIGHTHAWK'S GOLD. New York: Dodge, 1939.

Leithead, J. Edward. BLOODY HOOFS. New York: Ace Books, 1959.

Low, Glenn. VIRGIN BOUNTY. Chicago: Novel Books, 1959.

Lutz, Giles A. MY BROTHER'S KEEPER. New York: Ace Books, 1975.

McCulley, Johnston. GOLD OF SMOKY MESA. New York: Gateway, 1942.

McLeod, Tex. GUNS OF GILA VALLEY. London: Gaywood Press, n.d.

Martin, Charles M. THE DEUCE OF DIAMONDS. New York: Greenberg, 1937.

———. GUN LAW. New York: Arcadia House, 1941.

———. GUNSMOKE BONANZA. New York: Arcadia House, 1953.

———. TWO-GUN FURY. Hasbrouck Heights, N.J.: Graphic, 1954.

Miller, Tevis. BULLION ON THE RANGE. New York: Phoenix Press, 1937.

Nye, Nelson. CARTRIDGE-CASE LAW. New York: Macmillan, 1944.

———. MULE MAN. New York: Doubleday, 1988.

———. WILD HORSE SHORTY. New York: Macmillan, 1944.

Olsen, James P. THE CURSE OF THE KILLER. New York: Dodge, 1941.

———. POWDERSMOKE PADDY. New York: Dutton, 1939.

Piper, Anson. BLACK CREEK BUCKAROO. New York: Morrow, 1941.

———. THE PAINTED GHOST. London: Swan, 1946.

Reardon, Joseph. THE CERRO LOBO. New York: Phoenix Press, 1941.

Reilly, William K. RANGE WAR. London: Stanley Paul, 1940.

———. SECRET OF THE RANGE. London: Jenkins, 1946.

———. WAR ON THE LAZY-K. New York: Phoenix Press, 1946.

Repp, Ed Earl. COLT COURIER OF THE RIO. London: Ward Lock, 1952.

———. CYCLONE JIM. New York: Godwin, 1935.

———. GUN HAWK. London: Wright & Brown, 1937.

———. HELL ON THE PECOS. New York: Godwin, 1935.

———. HELL'S HACIENDA. London: Wright & Brown, 1951.

———. SUICIDE RANCH. New York: Godwin, 1936.

Rigoni, Orlando. CLOSE SHAVE AT POZO. New York: Lenox Hill, 1970.

Riley, Tex. GUNS ON THE RANGE. London: Wright & Brown, 1942.

————. GUNSMOKE RANGE. London: Wright & Brown, 1938.

————. RANGE JUSTICE. London: Wright & Brown, 1943.

————. THE SHOOTIN' SHERIFF. London: Wright & Brown, 1940.

Roan, Tom. GAMBLERS IN GUNSMOKE. New York: Abelard Press, 1952.

————. GUN LORD OF SILVER RIVER. London: Wright & Brown, 1943.

————. RAWHIDERS. New York: Zenith Books, 1958.

————. SMOKY RIVER. New York: Godwin, 1935.

————. WHISPERING RANGE. New York: Alfred King, 1934.

Rodney, George B. THE SECO BONANZA. New York: Phoenix Press, 1942.

Rud, Anthony M. THE SENTENCE OF THE SIX GUN. New York: Doubleday, Page, 1926.

Scott, Bradford. THE COWPUNCHER. New York: Gateway, 1942.

Scott, Leslie. BRANT OF TEXAS. New York: Arcadia House, 1960.

————. THE BRAZOS FIREBRAND. New York: Ace Books, 1953.

Shaffer, James. SLEUTHS OF THE SADDLE. New York: Phoenix Press, 1942.

Shott, Abel. THE BULLET BRAND. New York: Phoenix Press, 1947.

Small, Austin J. THE FROZEN TRAIL. Boston: Houghton Mifflin, 1924.

Strange, Oliver. SUDDEN TAKES CHARGE. New York: Doubleday, 1940.

Tompkins, Walker A. BORDER BONANZA. New York: Phoenix Press, 1943.

————. THE BORDER EAGLE. New York: Phoenix Press, 1939.

————. THE SCOUT OF TERROR TRAIL. New York: Phoenix Press, 1944.

————. THUNDERGUST TRAIL. New York: Phoenix Press, 1942.

————. TROUBLE ON FUNERAL RANGE. New York: Phoenix Press, 1944.

Turlock, Charles. DESPERADO. New York: Phoenix Press, 1941.

Tuttle, Gene. IMPOSTORS IN MESQUITE. New York: Ace Books, 1969.

Vane, Norman Thaddeus, and Rude, R. THE CAVES. Canoga Park, Calif.: Major Books, 1977.

Wallmann, Jeffrey M. Bronc: Brand of the Damned. New York: Leisure, 1981.

Ward, Brad. The Baron of Boot Hill. New York: Dutton, 1954.

————. The Spell of the Desert. New York: Dutton, 1951.

Westland, Lynn. King of the Rodeo. New York: Phoenix Press, 1941.

————. Prentiss of the Box 8. New York: Phoenix Press, 1943.

————. The Range of No Return. New York: Phoenix Press, 1939.

Westland, Lynn. Shootin' Iron. New York: Phoenix Press, 1942.

————. Trail to Montana. New York: Phoenix Press, 1943.

White, Samuel Alexander. Called Northwest. New York: Phoenix Press, 1943.

————. Code of the Northwest. New York: Phoenix Press, 1940.

————. Northwest Crossing. New York: Phoenix Press, 1944.

————. Northwest Law. New York: Phoenix Press, 1942.

————. Northwest Patrol. New York: Phoenix Press, 1943.

Willoughby, Lee Davis. The Gunfighters. New York: Dell, 1981.

————. The Rough Riders. New York: Dell, 1984.

Short Fiction

Adams, Stuart. "The Arizona Kid." *Spicy Western,* November 1936.

Anthony, Saul. "Gunsmoke Medicine." *Western Action,* May 1959.

Grey, Romer Zane. "The Raid at Three Rapids." *Zane Grey Western Magazine,* November 1970.

Griffin, Andrew A. "Johnny Forty-five's Iron Trail." *Wild West Weekly,* July 4, 1936.

————. "Ruin to Renegades." *Wild West Weekly,* January 31, 1942.

————. "Where Sheriffs Fear to Tread." *Wild West Weekly,* April 18, 1942.

Henderson, George C. "Quick-trigger Luck." *Wild West Weekly,* June 20, 1936.

Leslie, A. "The Texas Ranger." In Western Thrillers, ed. by Leo Margulies. New York: Robert Speller, 1935.

Roan, Tom. "Reformation of the Two-Man Wild Bunch." *Dime Western,* March 1941.

Steele, Francis. "The Sonora Ghost Rides." *Spicy Western,* November 1936.

182

Six-Gun in Cheek

Tompkins, Walker A. "The Renegades of Robber's Roost." *Range Riders Western*, March 1947.

Nonfiction References

Bonham, Frank. "Tarzana Nights." *Mystery Scene #17*, 1988.

Cancellari, Mike. CHECKLIST OF WESTERN AND NORTHERN FICTION, 1900–1980. Privately printed by the compiler, 1986.

Carr, Nick. THE WESTERN PULP HERO. Mercer Island, Wash.: Starmont House, 1988.

Coburn, Walt. WALT COBURN, WESTERN WORD WRANGLER: AN AUTOBIOGRAPHY. Flagstaff, Ariz.: Northland Press 1973.

Croy, Homer. "Country Cured." WRITER'S 1944 YEAR BOOK. Cincinnati, Ohio: Writer's Digest, 1944.

Dinan, John A. THE PULP WESTERN. San Bernardino, Calif.: Borgo Press, 1983.

Drew, Bernard. LAWMEN IN SCARLET. Metuchen, N.J.: Scarecrow Press, 1990.

Estleman, Loren D. "Beds & Bullets: Sex and Violence in the Western Novel." Western Writers of America *Roundup*, March 1983.

Goulart, Ron. CHEAP THRILLS. New Rochelle, N.Y.: Arlington House, 1972.

Holland, Steve. THE MUSHROOM JUNGLE. Westbury, England: Zeon Books, 1993.

Jones, Daryl. THE DIME NOVEL WESTERN. Bowling Green, Ohio: Bowling Green University Popular Press, 1978.

McDermott, Larry. "Meet Bill Claussen." Western Writers of America *Roundup*, January 1955.

Margulies, Leo. Introduction to WESTERN THRILLERS. New York: Robert Speller, 1935.

Martin, Chuck. "For 50 Old Timers." *Writer's Digest*, March 1942.

———. Letter to the Editor. *Writer's Digest*, December 1941.

———. Letter to the Editor. *Writer's Digest*, February 1943.

Pronzini, Bill. "Australia's Western Giant." Western Writers of America *Roundup*, November 1982.

———. GUN IN CHEEK. New York: Coward McCann, 1982.

———. Introduction to WILD WESTERNS. New York: Walker, 1986.

Pronzini, Bill. "On Collecting Westerns." Western Writers of America *Roundup*, September 1987.

———. "A Sense of History." Preface to WESTERN FICTION CATALOG 62. Minneapolis, Minn.: Dinkytown Antiquarian Bookstore, 1994.

———. SON OF GUN IN CHEEK. New York: Mysterious Press, 1987.

———. "The Western Pulps." THE BEST WESTERN STORIES OF BILL PRONZINI. Athens, Ohio: Swallow Press, 1990.

Robertson, Frank C. "Tom Roan: In Memoriam." Western Writers of America *Roundup*, July 1958.

Sadler, Geoff (ed.). TWENTIETH CENTURY WESTERN WRITERS: SECOND EDITION. Chicago and London: St. James Press, 1991.

Sonnichsen, C. L. FROM HOPALONG TO HUD: THOUGHTS ON WESTERN FICTION. College Station, Texas: Texas A&M University Press, 1978.

Strong, Charles S. "The Circulating Library Novel—What It Is and Where to Sell It." WRITER'S 1939 YEAR BOOK. Cincinnati, Ohio: Writer's Digest, 1939.

Tompkins, Walker A. " 'Just Another Western.' " *Writer's Digest*, April 1940.

———. "Plotting the Western Story." *Writer's Digest*, March 1939.

———. Letter to the Editor. *Writer's Digest*, July 1945.

———. Letter to the Editor. *Pulp 12*, Summer 1980.

Vinson, James (ed.). TWENTIETH CENTURY WESTERN WRITERS. Detroit: Gale Research, 1982.

Weiss, Ken, and Goodgold, Ed. TO BE CONTINUED... New York: Bonanza Books, 1972.

White, Samuel Alexander. Letter to the Editor. *Adventure*, April 15, 1935.

Zinman, David. SATURDAY AFTERNOON AT THE BIJOU. New York: Arlington House, 1973.

Index